Man Alive!

Living Spiritually in a Suffering World

Melanie D. Davidson

PublishAmerica
Baltimore

First printing

ISBN: 1-4241-3757-8
PUBLISHED BY PUBLISHAMERICA, LLLP
www.publishamerica.com
Baltimore

Printed in the United States of America

This book is dedicated to God.
The Love, the Light, and the Power of Freedom
in all that is good.

Special thanks to Jon Davidson, for his never ending
patience, support, love and fervent belief in the
"guiding light."

Chapters

Words of Light

I could write my thoughts down concerning the future,
But, why should I tell of the negative to come?
I could speak of the wrath of God and the day becoming night,
But, why would I want to discourage the Godly?
I could listen to only phrases of lost hope,
But, where is the faith in all of that?
I could tell of prophecies as a prophet of old,
But, the days of yore have not forsaken their words,
I could tell of times to come, and turmoil's test,
But the meek would find no strength in that,
I could scream out about the darkness of earth,
But a light would fade out from the hopeful hearts,
I could bring you a message of gloom and despair,
But your world would not glimmer with trusting abound,
I could tear down your spirit with shouts of the end,
But where would that leave you my follower, my friend.
I could sing but a song with a lark's melody,
But would this world allow your listening to me,
I could tell of you of hopeful, long lasting days of light,
But you must take off your sad shades, and look into my eyes,
For there you will find truth, and a promise fulfilled,
No doomsday forewarnings, just hope down the road.
So look into light, holding fast onto faith,
You will not be forsaken, nor your hope ever taken.
In your Godliest of hearts, find the truth never shaken.
And when you see days which are dark and foreboding,
The heaven inside of your heart shall awaken.

Melanie Trondson
12/11/06

Introduction

At this time in the world, it is interesting to look at how far man has come and how far he has also pulled back spiritually. It is important to look at our own individual lives and the effect our lives have on others'. The goodness we generate penetrates into the lives of those whom we come across on a daily basis and this is as it should be. We have much to be grateful for. We still have so much beauty on this planet and we have people who emulate angels on this earth. It is crucial to remember that no matter how bad things seem, there is a veil of goodness that blankets the earth. We are threads in God's tapestry. A tapestry woven together of many godly threads, each serving their own purpose, but together with other threads creating the most beautiful of all deitous quilts. It is a time of fear, worry, distress, confusion, bewilderment, sadness and forlornness. It is also a time of learning to let go. Should the people of this world learn to let go of the negative and focus on the positive, then we will see positive changes come about. It is in the positive force that we are able to ford on with hope. Hope changes darkness and turns it into light. Hope rekindles peace and kindness, beauty and faith in all good things. Godly priorities seem to have fallen by the wayside but there is still time to bring it all back, using prayer, using the heart and teaching others by speaking out about faith.

Man Alive! is a book written to inspire and teach others about walking a spiritual path in a world filled with so much suffering. Though we all seem to be living on earth, so many are dead in the spirit of Jesus. We need to survive here, together, with our friends, our families; however, we need to do so much more than just survive. The Lord never intended for us to come to earth and merely survive, his intention was for us to LIVE! To be able to find joy in our lives, to find laughter and happiness. He didn't want us to sit back and worry, fear and contemplate our futures by dwelling on dysfunctional pasts. Though there is much to learn from our pasts, God wants us to focus on today and what this very moment can bring to us. In all moments, there is a thing of beauty and goodness to be shared and to be made aware of. No matter our suffering, our financial stress, our broken hearts or broken relationships, there is still light around us if we should choose to open our hearts, eyes and ears to recognize.

Before reading onward, say a prayer that God opens your heart to all that is written in this book so that it can be of positive effect in your life. Much of what I write about you may have heard time and again in church or by your friends, but there should never be a cessation of the positive. Repetition is a good thing where the renewal of faith and hope is concerned.

My hope in writing this book is that there will be a light turned on in the hearts of those who may be walking through their lives with a feeling of dread, worry, darkness and dead-end streets. To lighten the load of those who spend much of their lives in what seems like a dark forest with little light. There is a way out and it all starts with a prayer and willingness to learn and grow. May God lift you up and out of your old life, into a life filled with faith, love and hope. God's blessings upon you always.

In the Beginning

In the beginning, God created the heavens and the earth. Most people know how that story goes. But did you know that in the beginning God also had YOU in mind? Long before your soul was even created, God had a plan to create you. Yes indeed, he jotted the idea of YOU down in his daytimer. He didn't schedule an appointment over YOU, he kept you there and when the time was right, and it came upon him, YOU were created, heart and soul. You are unique, different from all other souls on earth. It may seem sometimes that your thoughts are similar to others' thoughts, and what you see is what others see and what you feel, so do others. Yet, you are unique as each snowflake differs in form from another. You are also very special in the eyes and heart of God. From the tips of your toenails to the end of each strand of hair, you are a unique and blessed individual created by God to be a special part of the world and a very special part of the life of God himself.

God thinks about you all the time. He watches and is aware of everything you say, do and think. He is there from the time you rise in the morning, throughout your day and then watches you crawl into bed at night and when you are deep asleep, he is there watching over you and lives inside of you. Yet, how many times do you think about him?

When I was growing up, I went to Sunday school. My mother and father made sure that I got to the church and learned about Jesus. It was a great education, a very important education. In fact, perhaps the greatest education a child could obtain, and I carried it with me. Although my siblings and I would have rather stayed at home and played on Sunday, eventually, as I grew older, I came to realize why my parents were intent on taking us to Sunday school. They wanted to build a foundation. The greatest structures on earth are built with a firm and sturdy foundation. The same holds true for the heart. It needs a firm foundation as well. Many people today have foregone the idea of sending their children to Sunday school. Many do not realize the importance of it. If you think about it, God must really feel awful about this! He took the time to come to earth as a man, teach people about faith and how to live godly lives; sacrificing his own life on earth through crucifixion, and was resurrected so that all would be forgiven of their sins. Still, so many blow this off as if it were not a big deal. If YOU were not important to him, he wouldn't have made this move so long ago. Each and every individual deserves to learn about Jesus, and each and every individual deserves a shot at learning about his own spiritual heart and how God can work in his or her life. There must be a foundation and there must be a willingness to learn. It is up to the parent to do the work for the child by getting them to Sunday school so that the foundation can be laid. If for some reason you cannot get your child to Sunday school, then teach in any other way you can. Your child deserves to learn about Jesus.

Okay, so you may not have had the opportunity to attend Sunday school as a child, and you haven't participated in church, no problem. There are ways to learn without necessarily attending church. There is always time to learn more about God. It is never too late. Also, I have never believed that the way to salvation is attending church. There is so much talk in the world about this. Go to church and be saved! This is not always the case. Church is designed as a method for worshipping, congregating and educating, but it is not the final shape of the heart, nor is it the gate to heaven. Your heart is. With so many religions to choose from, and with so many different denominations, how does one go about deciding what is best for one's own spirit? You may choose to not attend at all. So be it. Let's go on to talk about spirituality. Spirituality is not religion. There are no laws, no doctrines, no set method of worshipping in spirituality, but there is one common bond between the two—God. Spirituality is the rediscovering of God in your heart and putting into play the connection between you and God.

We are all living in a world made up of so many different cultures, different races, different opinions and views. Each of us has pondered the thought of "what is right?" Which view is right, which religion is the right religion? What is the real truth about God? Believe it or not, each one of us may obtain the answer in their heart, where all truth lives. If God lives in one's heart, then there is the truth. Right there in the innermost reaches of one's heart. We all have choices to make here on earth. We can choose a religion and attend our favorite church, congregate and worship with our family, friends and strangers. We can also worship God in a way that is personal. By this I mean, coming to know God in all aspects of life, in all aspects of our experiences. Truth be told, it is far more important to recognize God in this way rather than just an hour a week in church. There are many who attend church and go about their daily lives in a very deitous way, and there are some who attend church and throughout the remainder of the week live as though they have no sense of God in their lives and heart whatsoever. One should remember to revere God throughout the rest of the week, in all ways, in all experiences, with all of one's senses. God is not just a Sunday event. He should be held in one's heart as first and foremost at all times. God is not an event that should be penciled in on our calendars or thought of as something we HAVE to do each week as though he were an inconvenience. Some people go to church on Sundays because they feel guilty if they don't. Some people go to church on Sunday because they have been told their entire lives they have to do this in order to be saved. This is not true. Revere God in all ways and at all times, not just on Sundays. He deserves your respect and your heart. You will be saved by your faith and your faith in God is something to live by every waking moment. After all, God has faith in you every waking moment.

There is not a single soul living on this earth today that can deny the fact that this world is in turmoil. Why? What has happened to the world? We still have racism, we have poverty and the hungry, we have war and hate, and we have an earth that is suffering in its diminishing natural resources. We have political dissention, bigotry, double standards, hypocrisy, high crime rates, more disease, more famine, natural disasters by the score. It is true that the rich are getting richer and the poor are getting poorer. Over the period of thousands of years, one would think that things could only get better, yet all of the abovementioned are as rampant as ever. In the United States, the health care costs are astronomical, many cannot find good-quality health care and the conditions here are not getting better, seems there is no way out. The cost of living for most people outweighs the salary. There is such an imbalance right now it is no wonder people are seeking help for stress disorders.

This is a stressful world we are living in! People are in such a big hurry to get to their destination, that it has become a *me, me, me* world. An attitude has formed and it isn't pretty. The world is full of fear and it has become a worldwide epidemic. Fear of the loss of jobs, fear of war, fear of an unstable economy, fear of one's neighbor, fear of not keeping up, fear of financial loss, illness, and terrorism. Satan loves this. Satan is having a heyday right now because he can see how people are slipping into his grasp. Satan preys on fear. The more the world fears, the more Satan reigns. So what now? Where is this world headed? It sure doesn't seem like there is anything just one person can do to change the ways of the world, or is there? Just one person. Multiply this by nine billion and the world will be changed. Nine billion people! The number is astounding!

Man alive! How can we get nine billion people to feel the same way, to rise up against fear and conquer it? How in the world can we get this many people to come together? Surely there would be heaven on earth if all people could come together in harmony, and agree on things. Surely we could figure out a way to conquer all of the things that we so consistently fear. Realistically, there is no way that we can get this many people to come together because of differences of opinions and views. One thing holds true, however— all it takes is one spiritual person to teach another, and then that person teaches another, and so on. The domino effect. After all, isn't that why God sent us here? To help each other? So all could learn about loving, giving and forgiveness? I believe so. Everything else is minute compared to these three things. Teaching and sharing is what is needed on earth right now. With these two things in mind and heart, we can make positive changes in the world, together. It cannot be just me, it cannot be just you, it must be us, together.

When I started to write this book, I questioned myself. I had frequented a local bookstore and walked to the section where they displayed all the spiritual books and I was astounded! Man alive! I just stood there looking at all the titles and all the authors whose names I did not recognize. I thought, *How in the world will my book ever make it out into this jungle of spiritual books? Why would God want my book in the market when it seems as though so many other authors have capitalized on the teaching of godly things?* I questioned over and over again in my mind, *What in the world can I possibly do to make a difference on earth? Will God use one of my books? It certainly seems as though God has all his messengers of faith in place and why would he need me to write? After all, look at all these books! Look at all the different books on all the different religions! Look at all the books on God and spirituality! Look how many people God has working for him!* It was very intimidating standing there questioning my place in the world and wondering if I was worthy as the others, enough so to get my own book published. On the other hand, why not me? I realized that maybe there are not *enough* people reading or writing about God, nor enough people teaching about God. In comparison to how many human beings there are on earth, sadly, the messengers of faith are actually a very small percentage. So, I knew I needed to write, to share with people thoughts on God. To do my best to teach them how to walk a spiritual path. Knowing full well that in this book writer's market there is much competition; after all, there are about a million other authors out there writing on the same subject. There would be competition. The thought of that put fear in my heart…the same thing I wanted to talk to people about ridding in their own lives. Then the Lord spoke to my heart and said, "Fear not, for your book will be published and read." That is all

I needed to hear. I was not writing a book in order to obtain my own glory in becoming a great author, nor was the reason my desire to obtain financial success. I was writing to teach and my *fear* was based on Satan's desire. He wanted me to fear not being successful and to fear the other authors who are successful. He didn't want this book to come out! So I sat down at my computer and started typing, relying on God to bring forth the words, paying no attention to my apprehensions, and thus, they went away. God also told me that it didn't matter if one person read this book, or a million, as long as I was spreading a message of hope to others. If this book gets into the hands of but one, that is good enough for God. All it takes is ONE. If all people realized that they are that ONE, then dreams of a heaven on earth will also be realized. One. You. All right then, it is time to get started.

Remembering Your Heart

Not so long ago, you were a baby. How cute and sweet you were! God remembers this as if it were just a few short minutes ago. How much do you remember about your youth? You more than likely do not remember your first steps, nor your first tooth, or reciting your first words. Most people can remember back to the age of five, some even further back. The furthest back I remember is the age of three. I remember that my mother had a meeting with a friend and took me along with her to her friend's house. I believe it was the middle of the afternoon and I was taken to a backroom and placed in a crib. Naptime? I couldn't believe that she was putting me in a crib and making me take a nap! I wasn't tired and I thought that I was too big for naps! I remember my mother shutting off the lights in the room but there was still enough light in the room to see the faint view of pictures on the walls and a bed and dresser. I was so angry with my mom, although I didn't scream and throw a temper tantrum. I was being a good little girl but inside, my heart felt as though I had been treated unfairly. This was my first hurtful memory and perhaps the only memory I have of being under the age of five. What did I do while I was in that crib? Did I fall asleep? I believe I eventually did, I don't really remember! What I do remember is that I stayed in that room and talked with

God about things. If I were asked what the conversation was about, I can't recall word for word, but I remember sitting in that crib and telling God how I felt and how unfair it all was that I was abandoned and left alone in this stranger's room. That is pretty much the extent of what I remember. I will always remember God's presence and how he was listening to me the entire time I spoke with him. I never felt alone. I was communicating with God through feelings. Did I hear anything back? Yes, and no. Not in the way one normally hears words spoken to them, but I remember the feeling of being assured of having God's company. There I was, this little girl sitting in a crib and talking with God. Of course, my vocabulary was pretty much nill, but in my heart my vocabulary spoke volumes. My earliest memory was one of God. My earliest memory was one of communication through emotion. This is how God works in our lives. When we are aware of God in our lives and our focus is on him at all times, we find ourselves more at peace, and a lot less angry about things. We become one with God in emotion and thus, he communicates with patience and love, and we in turn reflect this. This is what others see in a godly person. Patience, kindness, love, all positive emotions.

In your own life, do you remember the first time you had a spiritual experience? How far back can you remember? Was it an experience of God?

Children are what God refers to as "Heaven's Hope." There is nothing like the heart of a child. Nothing. Children are born on this earth and they learn, from the minute they take their first breath, they are learning creatures. Their eyes adjust to light and form, their brains teach them about sound and touch. But their hearts feel emotion from the instant they come into the world. The emotion of love, first and foremost. The warmth of their mother's and father's arms. They know that this is love. Babies know a lot more than most people give them credit for. It is crucial that they feel this love upon coming into the world, and it is of the utmost importance that they continue to feel this way throughout their growing years and into adulthood. There is nothing more important in the world than to nurture a child, love them and teach them about love. Love is God's special gift to the world and it starts from the moment of conception and on through earthly years. Children are untainted. They know nothing of sin, they know nothing of evil, they are pure. Their hearts come straight from heaven and they should be cherished. As children grow older and become a significant part of the larger world around them, they learn about evil, sin, and hate. They become as all people, a part of the world, and are heavily influenced by all around them. It is a sad thing actually, to see a child grow from being this innocent, pure creature, portraying so much goodness and heavenly spirit, to a child of the world. God knows what he is doing though, and there is no way a child can learn their lessons in life without being a part of it all. We have on this earth all the things we call evil, bad, or sinful, so that we can learn good. We must all learn forgiveness, so there are times we need to be forgiven. Children need to grow, which means that in their lifetime, they will experience heartbreak, sorrow, despair, depression, grief and sadness so that they will appreciate and learn about the opposite. They also need to learn about sin. Children must grow up and become a part of the world so that they can learn how to become once again a part of heaven. It is all about learning. Education is important and the greatest education comes from not just classroom time, but time among other people, so they may experience many varied emotions, which brings about many levels of learning. Love is the first emotion a baby feels, besides a sense of shock perhaps at realizing, *Hey, I am on the planet earth, what am I going to do now?!* Love is the first emotion and love should be the last emotion. All things in between are emotions designed to teach. There is truly a lesson in each and every emotion.

So you are all grown up now, and you find that life isn't all you thought it would be. You may be feeling fed up at the state of the world, fed up in your job, your home life, your relationships, your health and financial state. This, of course, is common and to be expected. After all, you are not living in heaven, or are you? A great deal of how we perceive the world and how we relate it to our own lives is based upon our spiritual heart. Wouldn't it be nice if we could all go back to being little babies and having others take care of us, hold and comfort us, feed us and protect us from this crazy world? That little piece of heaven that lived in us, where we felt secure and cared for, where we had others to rely on to make things just perfect for us. It sure sounds great, doesn't it? But it isn't possible because we are expected now to do that for our own children, grandchildren, and those who are elderly family members, or friends who count on us for support. We become not the children, but the caretakers. Meanwhile, this world goes on spinning around us and we become sensitized to the lives of others and their journeys. Sometimes it just seems to be more than we can take. We don't even remember the child that used to dwell within. In the age we all live in, it is important to remember our hearts. That little organ that beat in us as children and brought us into the world, that little special feeling of peace that we came to know upon our arrival in the world. Children are extremely connected to God, and when we are growing it seems that some of that wonder gets lost in the living of everyday life. We somehow lose that oneness with God that we felt while sitting in a crib in a dimly lit room. So, how do we get that back?

Prayer and awareness. Prayer is the key to becoming a child again, and a deep faith in God. Faith in God being the foundation. So, how does one go about learning faith or rekindling faith so that one can become a child once again? By believing in that which is invisible and powerful. We must remember our spiritual Father, for how can we be children without having had a father? The understanding is vital. We actually have never ceased being children, but what has happened through the years is we have become stressed out and fearful. Because of our experiences, we begin to think that we are the ones in control. We are not. We never have been. We need to relinquish the thought of *I am in control*. We are not, God is. He is our Father in heaven. He is the one who gave us life and in that redeeming thought we come to realize and focus on our faith. We learn eventually that what goes on around us is not something we are controlling and then acceptance comes into play. It is okay to not be the one running the world, it is okay to not be Superwoman or Superman, and it is okay to accept your own human limitations. About the only thing a person can control is their emotions. But even God will take over in this arena when asked in prayer. When a person is godly and keeps God as the ultimate focus at all times, this person will start seeing how he or she can sit back and relax a lot more, and let God do the rest of the work. Life becomes much easier and work no longer feels like work. This also allows for more time to pray, hug the ones you love, and also saves money on anti-depressants, antacids, and visits to the doctor.

To remember your heart means to remember from where you came. You came from an idea that God had. You came from this very divine being who decided that you were someone important. His thought was to place you on the earth so that you could learn, grow, teach and follow. To become one with him in all ways. You need to remember what it was like to fly a kite, to play, to be loved and to love. To laugh and rejoice in the innocence of who you are and were always meant to be. Your heart is the greatest asset you have because that is where the Lord lives. All people have God in their hearts, it is true, but not all people have God *living* in their hearts. Once you awaken to the child you once were, you will see that life is Disneyland forever. Life was never intended to be a living hell, life was intended to be heavenly. It is thus up to you to remember what it was like to be a child and pray to God to become as you were, always and totally free. Remember your heart always, as it is the finest tool God ever created.

Luke 18:16: *But Jesus called them to Him and said, "Let the little children come to Me, and do not forbid them; for of such is the kingdom of God".*

Prayer

Regardless of what you may have been taught on your religious journey in life, there are no rules pertaining to prayer. I emphasize this because it is important to understand that no matter how you connect with God, you will be heard and your words will not go unnoticed by him.

There was a time when I sat in a pew at a Presbyterian church and listened to the minister tell us how we should pray. In fact, I was singled out because during one of the prayers at this service I attended, instead of bowing my head and closing my eyes, I felt more comfortable keeping my eyes open, and was tilting my head toward the heavens. I believed I might see an angel hovering above the congregation in this beautiful sanctuary, and while lifting my eyes to the rafters above me, I listened to the minister's words and thanked God in my own heart for the blessings of the day. As soon as the prayer ended, the minister came right out and lectured with the words, "Those people who do not revere God by bowing their heads and closing their eyes during prayer are not paying attention." I knew he was talking about me. It made me feel small among the masses there. It was condescending and very insulting for he had no idea of the extent and sincerity of my prayer. It also made me think that he must have had his eyes open and

focused on the congregation while he was leading the praye
in order to see me, so wasn't this a bit hypocritical? I mean, h
wasn't even bowing his own head and closing his eyes.
stuck with me and left a real sore place in my heart, though
have forgiven this man because of the lesson I came to lear
from it all. The lesson being, no matter what any person tel
you, no matter their title and place in the church and in th
world, you must rely on your own heart for much of the trutl
The truth in this case being that if you do not close your eye
and bow your head during prayer, it does not mean the Loi
will not listen. If you know you are a godly person and ai
doing your best on earth, then trust what your heart tells yc
about things and don't always rely on what others say, r
matter their position in the world. Rely on what God says
you in your heart. God told me that when I pray, it is okay
keep my eyes open and my head tilted toward the heavens. A
a matter of fact, I have a picture of Jesus that hangs in m
bedroom and Jesus is kneeling down with his hands folded c
a rock in front of him. His head is tilted toward the heaven
and his eyes are beautiful and opened wide. He was no dou
communicating with God, his Father in heaven.

Prayer is the most deitous gift on earth and in heaven. Pray
is the most powerful gift on earth and in heaven. Prayer mov
mountains and is stronger than anything we can ever fathom.
is the most miraculous form of communication ever created.
is our connection to God and it is a rope that we cling to for hel
hope and happiness. The only time our prayers seem to fail
is when we let go of the rope. By this I mean we stop trusting
our prayers and thus cease our trusting in God. There is not oi
person on earth who hasn't let go of the rope at certain times
their lives but it is always there, dangling in front of u
Becoming one with God in our hearts requires us to hang on.

there a right way to pray? Jesus spoke of this when he was here on earth. He gave us the Lord's Prayer and it encompasses all that we should pray for to keep us moving along in our lives in a spiritual way. This prayer is common to most Christians. There are personal prayers though that pertain to our own personal struggles in life as well as the struggles and sufferings of others. There are also prayers for thanks to God. The "right" way to pray is by praying with an open heart, by being sincere, and by praying with trust. If we pray and are not convicted and are not sure our prayers will be answered, then we are doing ourselves and God a disservice. Why pray if you don't believe in your prayer and you don't believe it is being heard and will be answered? Some people are just not sure and this is where faith comes in. The stronger you are in your faith that your prayer will be answered, the more you KNOW it will be. It is a knowing, not just a believing that will bring about an awareness to how it is answered. For example, just this morning I was suffering from menopausal symptoms which were extreme. I was at my wit's end with it all because after having seen a few doctors for this, the blood work kept coming back showing little or no signs of hormonal imbalance. My body, however, was saying something completely different. I felt very much alone in this suffering because I needed a doctor's help and how could I get the help if the tests were coming up negative? The suffering included fatigue, depression, mood swings, sore body parts, anxiety and panic attacks, acne, dry skin, and the list goes on. This has got to be the worst suffering a woman can possibly endure! For the men out there reading this, I think some of you can relate because of having to live around a woman suffering from this malady. Unless you have lived through this it is hard to be sympathetic, but if you are one of the women living through menopause, you are NOT ALONE! This morning it

was all I could do to shuffle my feet through the kitchen to get a bowl of cereal to eat. Each lift of the spoon was a challenge, there was just no energy. I felt no joy, no happiness and wanted to crawl back into bed and cover my head up with my warm comforter, thinking that in a week's time this might all subside. Unfortunately, life goes on and I could not hide away. What I did was proceeded to my bedroom, sat on the edge of the bed and cried with all my heart and soul, all the while praying to God for mercy. There could have been a river running through my room for the tears that came. I had just gotten fed up and wanted to once again be my happy, upbeat, positive self and I prayed for about five minutes to be relieved of this suffering. I prayed with my entire being, all the while knowing God was hearing every single word I cried out to him. When the prayer ended, I remained on the bed with a hope in my heart and with a feeling of relief that I had just gotten a great deal out of my system. Then I told God thank you. I thanked him for listening and for answering the prayer, for not only did I believe he would, I KNEW he would. A few minutes later, energy started surging through my being as though a big brick was lifted from within my body. I felt lighter, my sadness subsided and I was left with hope and renewal. Would this last? That was my only thought. But a voice spoke to me from within saying, "This too shall pass." I may end up having more episodes of the menopausal symptoms, but for the time, they were lifted. I got up off the bed and started doing some housecleaning, all the while thinking, *I have been blessed.* Without suffering from this hormonal imbalance, how could I possibly learn what other women go through and how could I help them in the future had I not suffered from it all? There is a glorious lesson in the greatest of suffering and I was blessed enough to experience it. I was blessed to be healed of it as well.

Another experience regarding the healing power of prayer came to me just a week ago. I was in my kitchen making dinner and was suffering from a migraine. This is another painful experience and unless one has suffered from these tremendous headaches, there is no way to know how debilitating they really are. For the migraine sufferer, I can say, "There is hope!" While standing near the sink with my head pounding, I lost my patience and started stomping my feet heavily on the floor. I would just stand there stomping my feet in agony. I had already taken migraine medicine but it didn't seem to be working. Then I leaned over the sink with my head in my hands and just prayed so deeply that God would take this migraine from me. I prayed so deeply that I didn't move from that sink until I spoke to God from the innermost reaches of my soul. Before the prayer was over, I told God thank you, knowing that he would surely help me. I told him I KNEW he would help me. I didn't say that I believed he would help me, I said, "I KNOW you will help me." KNOWING is the crucial word here. You must KNOW that God can help you and believe in that knowing with all your heart and soul. At the end of the prayer I continued on with making dinner and my headache was removed instantly! INSTANTLY! This is not the first time he has healed me instantly but I think this was the first time I ever realized it instantly. Man alive! The power of prayer is awesome!

There is no end to what prayers can do in your life, but you must come to a knowing, not just believing that they can work for you. God is your friend, he wants what you want as long as it is godly and healing is godly. Whether you are praying for yourself or for someone else, pray with your heart and soul and KNOW that these prayers will be answered. Pray in your car on the way to work. Pray at work. Pray before, during and after eating your meals. Pray while you are watching television. Pray every single time you think of it as there is always something to pray for. I will tell you that God is your best friend and desires your conversation with him. If you are talking with him casually, that is a prayer to him! If you start a conversation where it seems you are doing all the talking and sometimes whining, GO AHEAD! He loves this! He loves any form of communication you take with him because when you do so, you are recognizing him in your heart. In a very special way you are telling him that you believe that he is there and listening to you. He doesn't care if you start out with "Dear God." He doesn't even care if you forget the "Amen" at the end of the prayer. These greetings and endings are minor compared to the fact that you are acknowledging him. It is, however, *respectful* to use "Dear God" and "Amen" in your prayers.

It is important to revere God. To place him above all else in your life. To worship him and remember he is KING. This is something we all must remember, that although he is like our best friend, we should remember to hold him in the deepest, most wonderful place in our hearts and respect and glorify him.

There was a Sunday when I sat in church and listened to the minister speak on revering God. He said that there was a little girl who approached him one time and told him that God reminded her of her grandfather. No doubt this little girl loved her grandfather deeply and held the warmest thoughts of him in her heart. The minister told the congregation that this was wrong. As I sat there with my mouth agape, the minister also went on to say that a man approached him one time and told him that God, to him, was like his old worn coat that always kept him warm in the winter and made him feel secure. This was no doubt a great coat to this man! Something he would never want to let go of. The minister told us all that this was wrong! He told us all that we should not revere God like an old, worn coat, or our grandfather, and he used a few other examples as well. I wanted to stand up that day in front of the three hundred or so people sitting in the pews and scream out about this, but I was raised to be polite and not make a scene in large groups of people so I abstained. How could this minister of faith tell all of these people how they should feel about God? I understood, however, that he was trying to get people to understand that people should revere God and place him on the highest pedestal of glory. I most certainly got his point, but at the same time wanted to reach out to these people and explain to them that there is not a single person on this earth who should tell another how they should love God. If you love him like he is a worn-out coat who has kept you warm and secure, that is fine. If you love him like a grandfather, that is fine too. As long as there is love, there is God. As long as there is God, there is love. God doesn't get all caught up in how you relate your love for him as long as you hold him dear in your heart and keep the love alive. Revering and loving are *almost* the same thing, loving is your feeling for him, revering is where you place him in respect to everything else in your life. Apparently, the man who loved his old, cozy, worn coat kept it close to his heart as it sheltered him from the cold, but probably just hung the coat up on a hanger and stuck it in the closet and it was forgotten about until he needed to wear it on a cold day. Did he revere the coat? Probably not. This was the minister's point, and after pondering this, I realized it was a good thing I did not stand up and make a stink about what he was telling everyone. He wanted people to know that God should be placed in a very glorious part of your heart, where you will not forget about him and where you will praise him for his blessings unto you. This is revering. Respecting.

In prayer, you can tell God how much you revere him and love him; in prayer, you can talk with him and listen to what he says back, in prayer you can go into the innermost reaches of your heart and become one with him. Before you can walk a spiritual life on this earth HE must be recognized. Recognize God in prayer and watch your life turn around.

If you take the steps toward a more spiritual life, you will start becoming more aware of the good and bad of the world and learn how to overcome. You will realize that you are walking this path with God and you are not alone. We are called upon to be like children in our hearts. Have you ever noticed that when children wake up in the morning, they are usually filled with an awe in their own living? They are not all caught up with the stresses of daily living, they are free to go about their day playing, laughing, and enjoying the wonders before them. This is how God wants adults to face life as well. Children oftentimes pray to God because they are taught to. But they also talk to God in their hearts in a way that is precious to Him. They do not always say, "Dear God," and commence with a prayer, they just talk to him by using their free and innocent hearts throughout the day. Children don't have any rules when it comes to their creator. They may not understand about spirituality, or religion, or any of their struggles to come, but they have a sense about them that is godly and good. We see God in their faces and we know that they are loved by God. Adults are also loved by God but because we have walked through life having to make choices and having to learn and become responsible, we are called upon by him in a deep way to pray to him for help. God knew life would not be a bed of roses but it can certainly be more fulfilling if we acknowledge him throughout our days. Remember your heart, for this is where he lives, remember to pray, for this is how we endure, communicate and thrive. Prayer is KEY in the beginning steps to a glorious life and is key throughout your entire journey on this earth. Why walk through life alone? Prayer is your connection to a fulfilling and glorious life with your best friend, your greatest love, your Almighty Father.

Jude 1:20-21: *20 "But you, dear friends, build yourselves up in your most holy faith and pray in the Holy Spirit. 21 Keep yourselves in God's love as you wait for the mercy of our Lord Jesus Christ to bring you to eternal life".*

Faith

What is faith? Is it something all people are born with? Is faith something that one learns as one walks one's path in life?

Faith is not just believing—it is knowing. It is a remembering of great things which cannot always be seen by the naked eye. Faith is an assuredness of security and a guiding light. Faith is knowing that in God, all things are possible. Faith is believing and knowing that there is a spirit who created us all and this being watches over us and lives within us if only we should call upon him and trust and believe in him. Faith is your eternity, for without it, there is no eternity. Faith is believing and knowing that God sent his Son to earth to teach us how to love one another. In turn he would die on a cross to take up our sins so that we may be forgiven by him and go on to reach a life eternal in heaven.

So, how does one acquire faith, or is it something we are all born with and perhaps forget about from time to time? How come some people are atheists and have no faith in God at all? How come it seems as though some people have always known faith and others have to learn it?

These are questions that are hard to explain, and the answer will vary from individual to individual. Many have different views on faith and how it comes into one's life and how it is learned. There are a great many religious faiths on earth and the common denominator in all faiths is the belief in a higher supreme being.

All children are born with faith. All children are born of heaven and thus are born with a heavenly faith. As they grow, mature and experience earth, many lose their faith. There are a great many people who see life through their own earthly eyes and thus those eyes become their heart. So, in essence, they become very earthly and the heaven that used to live in their heart diminishes a great deal. People become earthly and, because of this, lose their belief in the things that cannot be seen. For example, I have had a few people walk up to me and say to me, "I will believe in miracles in your life and my own when you show me the burning bush." I look back into the Old Testament of the Bible and read about all the miracles that apparently took place so many years ago. I question why angels aren't appearing to people like they used to. Mary, the mother of Jesus, had an angel appear to her bearing the news of her conceiving the Son of God. There were shepherds tending their flock by night who were confronted by angels telling them of the birth of Christ. Miracles happened to Noah, Moses, Paul, all of the disciples, yet it seems in this day and age, things like that just don't happen. We can read about the parting of the Red Sea, the Great Flood, the writing of the Ten Commandments, and many more miracles of major proportion that occurred a couple thousand years ago, but we are merely reading about them. It is up to our godly hearts to have faith in all of that but it is very, very hard for some people. Many people do not even believe in the Bible because they have no proof as to how it was written and they mention that it has been edited, translated and changed and that many of the books were left out of the Bible. How do we know there was really a burning bush that appeared before

Moses with God speaking through it? Sure sounds like a fairy tale. Man alive! Do those kinds of things really happen? Since they haven't happened to us, how do we know and how can we be sure? Faith.

Some people do not need proof of things, some people do. Some people are very pragmatic and scientific, while some people do not need scientific proof that miracles happen, that Jesus walked the earth, and that God is in his heaven and all is right with the world. This world would not be the same if we all believed exactly the same; it is best to keep an open heart and find happiness in the hearts of all people, for never will all people feel the same way in their spiritual beliefs and in their faith. What is truly important is to find your own faith through prayer and through awareness of the miracles that happen in your own life and then go on to teach others. I am not saying to cram your beliefs down another person's throat, there are methods to teach faith which are gentle and accepting. Even God does not want you to make people gag on your beliefs. God wants you to share your faith, knowledge and your experiences with others, and bring him into the picture in the most gentle of ways.

There was a time when I used to use the word "confidence" quite a bit. I would tell myself that I had the confidence necessary to work at a certain job, write my songs—anything pertaining to excelling and reaching my goals on earth. I claimed "confidence" as my stronghold. Through the years and my spiritual journey I have replaced that word with the word "faith." It was not so much my confidence that got me through in life, it was my faith that did. *Confidence* was my belief that I could conquer my fears, my suffering, my struggles, and achieve my goals, *faith* was my knowing that I could. Faith is the part of the heart that knows, not just believes in what is real, what is right and what is important.

The spiritual heart is interesting. It is a treasure chest of glory. So many people walk through life without ever opening the chest. All it takes to tap into the treasures of the heart is a prayer to God. Once he hears you asking him if he will open your heart up, he will, so that you may experience the glory of the treasures that lie within. The treasure consists of answered prayers, blessings, truth, and knowledge. Once you pray to God and he opens up this treasure chest in your heart, your world will change without a doubt. Your experiences on earth will be filled with enlightenment, your awareness of godly things will enhance, your love for nature, people, animals and the world around you will increase threefold, and your focus will be more centered on that which God wants you to recognize so that you may learn your lessons on earth with a glorious grace. Faith is your knowing that God can make all of this happen. God does not want us to just believe in him, he wants us to KNOW he is real and he is there at our side, to assist in our walk through life, to bless us with feelings of love and to help teach us how to respect, forgive and love our fellow man. Without faith, these things cannot take place. Faith is an understanding and a knowing of what is real even though it may not be seen with the eye. It is seen with the heart. The heart does more than just feel; it sees, it speaks, it educates. Once people understand that the heart is more than an organ beating within, keeping us alive, and realizing that the heart can keep us alive in so many other ways, then they will understand so much more about faith. If you were a tree, then faith would be your roots. If you were a bird, then faith would be your wings. If you were a cloud, faith would be the wind that moves you along. You are a human being though and faith is your lifeline. Without it, you cannot truly live as God has intended for you to live. Do you want to be inspired? Practice faith. Do you want to become successful in your life? Practice faith. Do you want your suffering to diminish? Practice faith. Do you want the negativity in your life to subside? Practice faith. Do you want to find joy, forgiveness in your heart, love in your life? Practice faith. Do you want to learn how to deal with the pain in your heart? Practice faith. The best way to practice your faith is by talking to God. Pray to him, communicate with him, let him know that you know he is there by speaking with him throughout your day. In all your decisions, ask him to guide you, in all your suffering, ask him to heal you, in all of your endeavors, let God be your best friend, the love in your life, the reason that you are here on earth. Let it be God! Let God be your priority, your greatest love, and you will find things easier, smoother, happier, more joyous and indeed more glorious than you could ever imagine. Practice faith and you will realize more than ever that life is indeed worth living. What is faith? Faith is God.

Matthew 17:20—*He replied, "Because you have so little faith, I tell you the truth, if you have faith as small as a mustard seed, you can say to this mountain, 'Move from here to there' and it will move. Nothing will be impossible for you."*

Be as a Child

I mentioned in a previous chapter what it is like to remember your heart. In this chapter, the same holds true. It is vital to become youthful in your heart regarding all things, for if you grow old and your youth disappears, then your heart can harden like a rock. When this happens, one becomes cynical and distrusting, overly cautious and more critical of others. When God sends children into the world they have a trust that is unequaled to those who have seen their share of woes in this world. This world is not the happiest of places these days. Evil has made its mark and is alive and well in the media, computers, radio and television, schools, and as hard as it is to believe, even churches. The more spiritual you become, the more you begin to see this. Your awareness will grow and you will be able to depict the evil and the good more clearly. What is spiritually important is to be able to see the differences in good and evil and then choose with your youthful heart to be a part of only the good. Focus on the youth. Little children want to play. Little children see a dandelion as a flower. Little children love animals and they are filled with wonder. Little children laugh, blow bubbles, dance, sing and express themselves with the most carefree nature. Little children love God. They may not understand the idea of God, religion, or spirituality, but their hearts are his, and this is why they find happiness in the smallest of things. Their hearts have not been tainted. Their experiences are few and the majority of them are good, happy and loving. They stare the future in the face, not knowing what lies down the road, not realizing what experiences await them. They have hope for a wonderful life. This is godly! This is how God wants adults to feel...he wants them to hope and find happiness in the smallest of things around them.

There is something to be said for the aging adult. Along with the aging come all sorts of experiences, lessons and knowledge. It is one thing to have lived a long life having learned a great deal about the world, it is another to be able to take what one has learned and share it with others, and also find the good in all the lessons. There are a great many adults in the world who are wise beyond their years, but what makes them truly wise is how they have put their knowledge to use. What they have retained in all of their gainful experiences and how they go about spreading their knowledge is what makes them truly wise. There are advantages to being elderly and wise. The wise man or woman has the ability to pass on knowledge to the young to better his/her world. Many of the elderly become cynical though, and instead of passing on the knowledge so that others may grow to be wise, many will sit around and criticize the young and the world in its negative state. Growing older does not mean we need to grow old and become crotchety. It is possible to retain one's youth even in one's elderly years. Because the body must age, and the elderly person's body cannot move in the way it used to years ago, it is not always easy for an aging person to run, play, dance, sing and frolic as a child. They can, however, still sit with a child and empathize with a child's heart. They can still retain their youth by participating with children, and also by teaching children about God. They can set the example by putting themselves on a youthful level and seeing things the way children do. This brings to mind a poem I wrote quite a few years ago.

A Child

A child holds the key to the doors of the heart,
To the passage of life's sweet existence,
All we imagine and all we could be
Is seen in their youthful persistence,
Determined to capture a moment in time,
It flies much too quickly before them,
Let them be dreamers and hear what they say,
For too often, grown-ups ignore them.
Gentle pretending, their make-believe world,
Enhance the beauty around us,
We may pretend to be grown-up until
Their innocent laughter has found us.
A child holds the key to the doors of the heart,
To all that we hope for and treasure,
Nothing compares to their wondering eyes,
A child is the world's greatest pleasure.

A child holds the keys to the doors of the heart, to the passage of life's sweet existence. All we imagine and all we can be is seen in their youthful persistence. This is what God wants for us.

As one grows spiritually, one's youth comes back and one can see through a child's eyes. Children do not fear, they learn to fear. Children do not hate, they learn to hate. Children do not know much but they learn much. It is a sad thing, yet true.

Children become earthly and learn about the woes of the world as they grow, they learn from watching their parents, they learn from their peers and they learn from what they are exposed to on a daily basis. We cannot shelter children from this learning, but we can teach them about their own spiritual nature as they grow. There are just as many good things in the world as there are evil things; in fact, more. Focusing on positive, good things has become harder and harder for all of us to do because of our exposure to the bad. Turning on the news at night is a good example. We hear about so much bad happening in the world and thus we are sensitized to the bad. Even going to the grocery store can be a horrifying experience as we are exposed to all sorts of people from all walks of life, who love and hate in different ways. Instead of focusing on the people who shove their cart into yours, why not focus on the man in the bakery who offered your child a free cookie? Which person is your child going to focus on? Of course the man in the bakery.

Evil begets evil. The more a person's thoughts are focused on revenge, hate, unforgiveness, distrust and the judging of others, the more it will come to him. What you put into the world, expect the same back. It is also an interesting thing that when a child gets into a fight with another child, they are usually out playing together again the next day. Children can teach us much about forgiveness. As adults, instead of playing into the evils of the world, it is best to turn and walk away and not give in to it. When I talk about being as a child, I am speaking of retaining the love that you have for things which you may have turned away from. When the treasure chest in your heart opens, and you find all the blessings that have been carried within it for so many years, you will automatically see your life through a child's eyes and heart. You will stop focusing so much on the evil of the world and focus more heavily on the good. This is not only a good thing for you, it is a good thing for your children, and a very good thing for your grandchildren for they will see you as a very loving and happy mentor. Another way of retaining the childlike side of your heart is to pray continuously. Instead of cussing out the tailgater behind you, pray for this person for they need to learn a very valuable lesson and they will, one day. Instead of harboring hate inside your heart for your neighbor with the barking dogs and the parties that last until four o'clock in the morning, pray for them to learn about this and God will teach them about their inconsiderate nature in his own way. God has ways of making things work, all you need to do is pray. Instead of begrudging your micro-manager boss, who throws negatives at you constantly, pray for this boss so that he too will learn his lessons on earth. We all have lessons to learn, each one of us. This is why we came to earth, to learn and to love. I would hope that if I have made an error in my driving, the person in the car whom I have upset would pray for me instead of giving me rude hand gestures. Wouldn't it be nice if every time someone was wronged, they would pray instead of throwing their vengeful and hateful hearts toward someone else? I am sure we would find peace on earth then, but for now, it is time to learn, learn and learn some more.

Be as a child. Let go and let God. Forgive and find joy in the world. Turn away the ugly and focus on the beautiful. Pray and allow God to work in your life to bring back the child in you that may have been forgotten long ago. There exists a child within us all and it is time to rekindle that fountain of youth which can bring about more happiness, laughter, glory, joy and more love than we can even imagine. Pray and let God bring this child forth.

Matthew 21:15-16—*15 But when the chief priests and the teachers of the law saw the wonderful things he did and the children shouting in the temple area, "Hosanna to the Son of David," they were indignant. 16 "Do you hear what these children are saying?" they asked him. "Yes," replied Jesus, "have you never read, 'From the lips of children and infants you have ordained praise?'"*

Mark 10:13-14—*13 People were bringing little children to Jesus to have him touch them, but the disciples rebuked them. 14 When Jesus saw this, he was indignant. He said to them, "Let the little children come to me, and do not hinder them, for the kingdom of God belongs to such as these".*

Matthew 18:1-4—*1 At that time the disciples came to Jesus and asked, "Who is the greatest in the kingdom of heaven?" 2 He called a little child and had him stand among them. 3 And he said: "I tell you the truth, unless you change and become like little children, you will never enter the kingdom of heaven. 4 Therefore, whoever humbles himself like this child is the greatest in the kingdom of heaven."*

Transformation

Transformation means change, conversion and in a spiritual sense it means to be born all over again. Say goodbye to your old life and hello to your new one. Should you choose to put into practice what you read in this book and follow the steps, you will see yourself move from caterpillar form into the form of a very beautiful and glorious butterfly. It will not be *your* doing actually, but the will of God. Should you decide to become a spiritual being in all its deity, you will find that you are not the one controlling your life or the life around you, but you will come to realize it is *God* transforming you. You, however, are the one that gives God the go-ahead. You are the one who says, "Lord, take me now into your hands and mold me, guide me and turn my life around." Then, as you put into practice positive and godly thoughts, God actually gets to do the rest. In fact, God is the one who blesses you with positive and godly thoughts. The easiest thing in the world to do is to live with God controlling your life. It is great because everything falls into place exactly as he wills it and all you do is relish in his love and thank him for it. Your awareness of beautiful things heightens, your recognition of self enhances, and you figure out that you have never been in control—God has been. It makes it easier for God when you let go and allow him to make the moves in your life. Your decisions become easier to make and you start gaining an understanding of why and how things are happening in your life. In your awareness you start to see that your prayers are answered exactly as he wants them to be and in his time. There is a dawning realization that everything is moving in a motion that is absolutely perfect. Even when mundane things go wrong in your life, it doesn't feel as though it is the end of the world, as it used to. Patience becomes a presence in your life, where it may not have been before. Forgiving others becomes easier and asking for forgiveness becomes a true blessing. You also learn to forgive yourself with greater ease. In this transformation, you will start sensing a calmness in your heart, when at one time it was hard to sit still for more than ten minutes without anxiety creeping into your being. You start realizing that death is a new beginning and that brooding about it is senseless. The knowledge of your existence on earth becomes clearer so that you can feel as though you are an intricate thread in a tapestry woven by God in such a beautiful way. In this transformation you learn to love as you have never loved before. You will discover newfound gifts that you never knew existed within. Heaven becomes your sidekick and the signs of heaven on earth become apparent. There will be signs you will notice which you never noticed before. Amazing things will start happening in your life and you will become blessed with deep feelings of hope and joy. All of a sudden, you realize that you are alive! Looking back on the old life is a given, for you remember who you were and now rejoice in who you are! Man alive! What a wonderful transformation! Even in your physical suffering and pain, you realize that there is a reason for it. There is a reason for all things. Your learning becomes a constant and everything you do becomes a lesson. There will be a focus on the why's, how's, and where's of everything. The reason your curiosity peaks in this transformation is because you have opened the treasure chest and are now exploring not only yourself, but the world around you. The answers to your ponderings reach out to you, instead of your searching endlessly for them. God thinks this is great because he has waited for you for quite some time, and now that you have allowed him to work in your life, he starts moving things along for you, with the greatest of ease, and your life becomes the most graceful dance. You have become peaceful, you have become an all loving being and you have become free. Free to live your life without restriction. It sounds perfect, but is life always going to be this perfect? Yes, and no. It is perfect in the sense that you are healed of your old life and free in your spirit because of God's love for you and your love for him and your faith in him. You will not be free of the world. You still need to live in a world that suffers. The difference is, you do not need to be a part of the world as you were. In this spiritual transformation you become very aware of the differences between heaven and earth. The higher you fly above the earth, the greater the gap between you and earthly things. There is nothing wrong with being in the world as long as you do not become a part of all the worldly things around you. You remember that you were a being born of heaven, and that once you were placed on this earth, you were subject to worldly ways. Becoming spiritual brings you out of the world and once again back into the arms of heaven, not in a physical sense, but in a spiritual sense. Going out and getting drunk on a Friday night doesn't hold the weight in your heart as it used to. Lusting for material possessions is no longer a priority. Envy and jealousies subside. Your tongue speaks godly words instead of words that pierce God's heart. Instead of lashing out at those who you feel are doing you an injustice, you feel a deep sense of compassion for them and their journey as well. Instead of saying foul things about your boss under your breath, you now find yourself praying for him or her. Instead of gossiping with your friends about others, you find yourself repulsed by even being around the gossip. Instead of pointing fingers at others, you start feeling a compassion for them and begin to pray for their spiritual growth. You find empathy swelling inside your heart for those who suffer and for those who have not transformed as you have and there will be an intense desire to bring them along with you. God is great, for he brings you into contact with those who share a similar transformation. He will surround you with angels of faith on earth who just happen to come into your life during this entire transformation. It is amazing! Man alive! I don't say this lightly. Man needs to be alive and so many are walking around dead in spirit. You, like many others, become the exception. Even your friends will notice the change in you, and some will have a difficult time with your goodness. Many will fear the change in you because even positive change can be a difficult thing for some to accept. It may throw your relationships into a spin for the old world is thrown away and a new one begins. Not to worry though, if your friends are true, good friends, they will embrace the change and they will see the example you set. It is a great chance for you to bring them along with you in all of your transformation. Sharing this metamorphosis is a very positive thing and goodness breeds goodness.

It is a suffering world in which we live. With war that seems endless, with hate and discrimination abounding, with bitterness and turmoil seeping into families, friendships, the workplace and in neighborhoods throughout the world, it is time for people to wake up and find their spiritual hearts so that together, we can put an end to this catastrophic hell on earth. It is time to transform not only ourselves, but share this transformation with the world. All people coming together with a faith in the Almighty, so that the world can finally find a peace, an everlasting love, the truest and greatest transformation ever.

So, what should you do to acquire this transformation? Pray. Ask God to open up that treasure chest that is your heart, and allow him to work in your life like never before. Allow the Almighty Lord to be number one in your life and you will always find the light on your path. You will always be graced with a lamp unto your feet and you will find yourself ALIVE!

John 3:3—*Jesus answered and said to him, "Most assuredly, I say to you, unless one is born again, he cannot see the kingdom of God."*

Listening to Your Heart

Part of the entire spiritual transformation process requires listening to your heart. Although the brain is the organ that enables you to think, your heart is the organ that guides the brain into the thinking process. Those who do not listen to their hearts will find themselves struggling and unceasingly trying to pull themselves out of the quicksand of life. Once you have asked God to guide you, in all ways, you will notice that you are pulled out of the quicksand and when you venture close to it, your heart will give you the warning signs. Listening to your heart requires an open heart. In other words, upon waking in the morning, say a prayer that God speaks to you throughout the day regarding all your decision-making and all your moves. In turn, God will speak to you in many different ways. There are times throughout the day that I will refer to as "thinking times." These are moments when you ponder what you should do regarding certain situations or times when you are alone in your thoughts and are pondering the how-to's in your life. These are times when you are taking a bath or are in the shower, washing dishes, driving to work, etc. Moments when nobody else is around and you have time to sort things out in your mind and heart. These are great times to listen to your heart. For example, let's just say that you are standing in front of your sink washing dishes and it is quiet, you start thinking about what you should do about a given situation. You start asking yourself questions. *How should I handle this? What should I do about this?* If you will ask the question and know that God is listening, he will answer and your decisions regarding the situation will come to you quickly. It may seem as though it is your own voice you are hearing but it is really God's voice speaking through you. Your decisions become God's decisions, and God's decisions become yours. You become one with God in this way. It is truly an amazing thing! You will start realizing that you are not alone and that God is walking through your life with you, in all your decision making. You will also notice that you can find things easier. There was a turning point in my own life where I realized that I had acquired a great gift for finding lost items around my house. About seven years ago, shortly after my own spiritual transformation, I was doing childcare out of my home. A little girl I cared for had taken off her shoes and placed them somewhere in or around the house. I frantically searched for the shoes and knowing her mother would be coming to pick her up soon, I was in a frenzy. I stood in the middle of the family room wondering what I was going to do about this situation and said to God, "Oh no God, I have no idea where Meghan's shoes are and I need to find them quickly!" All of a sudden a calm fell over me. As I stood in the middle of this room, even with all of the other children playing and toys scattered around me, a very calm voice from within said to me, "Be peaceful, trust me and I will guide you to the shoes." It was more a feeling than words but I trusted what my heart was telling me. The heart talks in "feelings," not just words alone. So, I stood there in the middle of this room with this calm feeling washing over me and then I started walking slowly up the stairs. I walked to the sliding doors that lead to the backyard and went outside and into the little kids' playhouse, where Meghan's shoes were waiting for me. I was stunned at first! *How did I do that? Wait, I didn't do that! God did that!* It was a miracle, and though it was not the parting of the Red Sea, nevertheless, it was a miracle that I was able to listen to my heart and be guided as I was. It was as if my body knew exactly where to walk. I had opened my heart and was led. Did God scream into my heart, "Mel, you need to go outside and get her shoes because they are in the playhouse!!?" No. It happened in the most peaceful way. Some would call this psychic. If listening to one's heart is psychic, then perhaps. A few days later, the daycare children were watching a movie and playing in the family room. When it came time for the parents to pick up their children, I noticed that one of the little boys did not have his socks on. What happened to his socks? I thought, *Uh oh, not again!* The case of the missing footwear! So, as I so often did, I started rummaging around in the toy box, looking under chairs, running up and down the stairs in dire search for the missing socks. Then, once again, I stopped what I was doing and stood in the middle of the family room and asked God to help me find the socks. I didn't hear any words, I just felt a peaceful calm from within and after standing there in this state for about five seconds, I turned around and walked over to the couch, lifted up the middle cushion and there were the socks! It was another miracle, and believe me, to a childcare provider, this is a miracle! Moms need to pick their children up with socks on their feet! It may not have been a miracle to some, but to me it was.

A few days ago, my boyfriend and I were watching television and we had lost the remote control. I started looking around the room and could not find this gadget anywhere! I then decided to put a log in the woodburning stove when a thought passed through me. *Mel, stay calm, trust, and you will be led to your remote control.* So, I closed the door to the woodburning stove and stood straight up in the living room. I casually walked over to the bookshelf to the right of the television set and there it was, on the shelf to the right of the television set. Amazing! Since I started listening to my heart in this way, I have found people's keys for them, and all sorts of misplaced items. I no longer run around in a tantrum searching for things. This is what I refer to as listening to the heart. Since I have been putting this into practice, I have also noticed that my reflexes have become extremely sharp. So sharp that I have freaked people out with how I catch things in midair. An item will be falling out of a cupboard above me and my hand is underneath the item before it has a chance to get midway to its destination. I have saved many drinking glasses this way. It is an interesting thing, because I do not have the time to sit and ponder and be calm as I do when I search for lost items. It is an instantaneous reaction. My senses have become acute. This is another example of listening to the heart, although the heart reacts for me, signaling to the brain that something is going to fall and as quick as lightning my hand is there before I even had the time to think about what was transpiring. Sometimes it even freaks me out! Man alive! *What is happening to me?!* I would wonder excitedly. It has all been a part of the spiritual transformation mentioned in the previous chapter.

Have you ever been in the grocery store searching for items with no idea what aisle they are in? Transform to the spiritual side and you will not need to worry about finding things in the grocery store ever again. It is a matter of opening up the heart, listening and trusting what you hear and how you are guided. One day, I was in Wal-Mart with a friend. We were looking to buy a pair of sunglasses. As we entered the building, my friend said, "Hmm, I think we need to go this way."

I said, "No, that is not the way, but God will guide us to the sunglasses."

My friend smiled and said, "All right," looking at me as if I were out of my mind.

I stood for a moment and then listened. This time, I did hear the words. Funny though, they sounded like my words, as if I were talking to myself, but I knew this couldn't be. I had no idea where the sunglasses were! This is what I heard. "Go straight. Now turn slightly to your left and then go right and walk down this main aisle. Keep going, keep going, now turn to the right on the next aisle. Keep walking, keep walking. Now in a couple more steps look to your right." Lo and behold, we were standing in front of the sunglasses stand. My friend didn't think much about this, but I sure did! How did that happen?! Instead of jumping up and down in the store and making a scene about what just transpired, we just took the sunglasses we wanted and proceeded to checkout. In my heart, I was thanking God profusely!

Since that time, I have gone into stores and have been led to what I need with perfect ease. In fact, yesterday, I was looking for Graham cracker crumbs and was perplexed. I had searched all over the baking aisle and could not find my crumbs! So, I said, "Okay, God, please lead me to my crumbs so I can get out of here and back home to cook dinner."

He said, "Turn around, and walk down the aisle and don't stop until I say stop." No problem. I kept on walking all the way down the aisle and saw the pudding mixes and then the crusts for pies and he said, "Stop!" I stopped. When God says, "Stop," you stop! He told me to look on the very bottom shelf and as I did, there was a lone box of Graham cracker crumbs that had been pushed out of view and was hidden by other boxes. The chance that I would have ever found this box of crumbs on my own was slim to none. I stood there in awe, thanking God for leading me and helping me once again to find something that I may never have found on my own. *Trust*. There must be trust that one can be led or one will not be led.

Listening to your heart teaches you about right and wrong. There are choices one must make in order to get through this life and we choose to listen or not listen. Last night as I was getting ready for bed I thought about how nice it would be to eat a couple of chocolate chip cookies. Being a diabetic, I needed to be careful and test my blood sugar to see if I was in the range to be able to do this. I am also on an insulin pump which I can program to lower my sugar levels. I had just baked these cookies and as they came out of the oven, the smell was intoxicating. I wanted to just jump right in and gobble them up. I listened to my heart and was told to test my blood sugar and I was a little on the high side. So, I took a couple of units of insulin to bring the sugar level down and was told to wait another hour to two hours before I could eat these cookies. Did I really want to stay up another hour just to eat a couple of cookies? Yes! When my blood sugars came into a perfect range, I ate the cookies and took the correct amount of insulin to compensate for the starch in the cookies. This took self discipline on my part and also a willingness to wait. Patience. I have not always been so disciplined. In fact, there are times when I do not listen to my heart and thus end up paying the consequences for my decisions and actions. It is much the same as a parent telling a child to not eat cookies before dinner. The child learns to be patient and wait for the cookies. As hard as it is, it is a lesson. Listening to the heart is a lesson and it takes discipline, patience, and trust. God knows what is best for us and teaches us if we only listen to him. Many people might say that this is our own conscious thought and our knowing what is right and wrong. It is the same exact thing, only I choose to use God. I could say that I was using my intelligence by testing my blood sugar knowing full well that a diabetic should not delve into eating sweets without testing their blood sugar levels. So be it. My own conscious thought and my intelligence comes straight from the heart of God. The heart of God lives in my heart, thus, we are one in thinking and decision making. We walk together, in all ways, and it sure has made life a lot easier.

Listening to your heart is a gift. It is a glorious blessing. It comes when we ask God for help and for his love to guide us in all ways. There are other ways God speaks to us, not just in help to find things we may need; he will talk to our hearts using our own feelings. When someone you know has been hurt in some way, God uses your heart to feel. God feels the same way as you do when something like this occurs. He will tell your heart to reach out to your friend and help them in any way you can. You may send them a card, flowers, a phone call or anything else that pops into your heart to make them feel better. It is empathy, giving, and it is God. Your giving nature comes from God and the more you tune in to God, the more your heart feels deeply for others and also for yourself. I am the type of person who always cries during sappy movies. I can cry during commercials too if they touch my heart in some sensitive way. In fact, I cry about many things but that is because I feel so deeply about things. I have been told in the past by friends and family members that I cry too much or that I am too sensitive about things. When I was younger this bothered me a lot as I was always taunted and teased about this. My heart felt so strongly about things that I just couldn't turn off the tears. As I grew older, and was still told I was too sensitive, I finally decided that it was all right to feel this sensitive; after all, I knew that God and I were one in heart and if I felt this way, then God must too, and that these feelings were good feelings. Now, when someone says that I am too sensitive, I tell them that it is too bad that they don't experience this intensity of feeling. No longer do I feel bad about feeling bad, or feeling overjoyed. Could you imagine walking around feeling nothing? I think that most people would rather feel something than nothing at all.

When listening to your heart, remember that God speaks to us in all matter of different ways. He may be the feelings you are feeling, he may use words that you hear from within you. He may be that urge that comes over you which reminds you to pick up some milk on the way home from work. He reminds us of things, he guides us into and through life, he calms us down and he confirms our joyous and godly feelings regarding the most sensitive parts of our hearts. He is our Father, our friend and the greatest voice ever. Listen closely to what God tells you and you will find peace in your life.

Matthew 7:7-8—7 *"Ask and it will be given to you; seek and you will find; knock and the door will be opened to you. 8 For everyone who asks receives; he who seeks finds; and to him who knocks, the door will be opened."*

Isaiah 58:11—*"The LORD will guide you always; he will satisfy your needs in a sun-scorched land and will strengthen your frame. You will be like a well-watered garden, like a spring whose waters never fail."*

Understanding the Hearts of Others

Assuredly I tell you, that if everyone on this earth thought of others more than themselves, in a very godly and righteous way, then this world would not be in the shape it is in today. Sadly, however, this is not the way of the world and there are a great many people in need of tuning in to the hearts of others. There are millions of people on earth who are very good though and those people will be blessed for their goodness. God does not forsake his godly children on earth. I am reminded of a song that was a hit back in the sixties—"What the World Needs Now Is Love." It was sung so many years ago and still to this day, what the world needs now is indeed love. It baffles me that there is still racism in this world. Racism is not a new idea, it has been an illness on this earth for a very, very long time. There are parents today, who had parents, and their parents before them, who encouraged and taught their children about racism. Through verbalizing their hate for others and teaching this to their children, it has become a trickle-down effect. It is taught to children who live in homes where words cut like a knife into the hearts of many. Even if these words and feelings are vocalized just in the home and not in public, the children pick up on them and they take the words to heart. The children will attend schools which are interracial, bullying words and actions come into play, and therefore leads to the condemnation of children who are undeserving of such hatred. The saddest thing of all is that these children who are under attack carry this plague with them and harbor deep feelings of resentment towards the group or individuals who attacked them through their days in school. Eventually, the children who were attacked become attackers as well. If they don't become bitter, they will still retain the memory of such an injustice. I blame parents for this, because it is the parents' responsibility to teach children that this type of behavior and these types of actions are unfair and should not be tolerated. Parents need to stop the name calling and cease the hatred if they want their children to grow up to be loving individuals who find peace in the hearts of all people. There is a way to stop the racism but adults need to learn and listen to their own hearts regarding such a matter. People have been trying to find a way to stop this for a great long time, but as surely as the war on racism has been fought, it continues on even to this day.

How are we going to stop this? On an individual basis, there is much we can do. By living a spiritual life, we can share our own hearts with others and teach by setting the example. It sure doesn't seem like much, but in truth, it all starts with one individual. If we can all be counted as that individual then the trickle-down effect comes into play and our teaching others becomes the rule. Take this book for example. Should you, after reading this book, find your spiritual self, then you may pass this book along to a friend who in turn gets the message which lies herein, and then they pass it along and so on. If you should choose not to pass on this book, then word of mouth is a fabulous tool. You can talk to others who have not learned about racism and unforgiving hatred. The domino effect has worked miracles in the lives of so many, just by simply passing on your godly lessons and how you have come to know God, you share with the world a great blessing and in turn God blesses you with a peace that is unequaled. It is faith in knowing that the good you do on earth comes back to you threefold.

Everyone is born with a heavenly heart. Each and every individual upon coming into the world carries with them a reminder of heaven. I don't think any of us have looked into the eyes of a baby and seen anything but love. Why don't we see this all the time when we look into the eyes of adults? Because their heavenly hearts have been tainted by the world and by circumstances which evolve around them as they have grown. Believe it or not, some people just don't learn about all of these things. So many adults feel that they are the ones in control and they go about their lives doing things that are ungodly and just don't even care much for their fellow man. It is the saddest thing on earth. We are here to learn, to love, to be educated about what is good *and* bad so that we can choose the good in all ways.

Not all people are bad people. In fact, the majority of people that I know and have come in contact with in my adult life are genuinely good people. I also know that since I rediscovered my own spirituality, God has blessed me and surrounded me with people who go above and beyond what so many people on earth say, feel and do. He has brought into my life very good people and yet, I still come in contact with so many who don't have a clue about other people's hearts. As a substitute teacher, I see this in the children in the high school where I work. So many are clueless about what it means to be godly and good to others. They are very focused on themselves, and of course, what teen isn't? The life of a teenager requires focus on what lies in the future and gearing up for the real world. However, what should be taught to the teenager is the focus on the hearts of all people, thereby generating within them a deep sense of empathy for the world around them. This is the best education for any teen, yet so many are focused on things which are not godly and which will not provide for them a godly future.

Teaching is key! We are not just souls sent to earth to walk blithely along, surviving only for ourselves. Our mission on this earth, each and every one of us, is to learn to love, and thus teach others about love. Without this teaching, there becomes a breakdown of the goodness meant for the world. God is watching all of us. How in the world can God do his work, if we will not allow him to? It is not merely us on earth, it is God with us as his tools. We are all tools and we are meant to be used by him although there are so many people who do not know this, do not understand this and have not been taught this. This is why it is vital for all people to learn about loving their fellow man, for if all people will learn, then all will have the potential to teach, which in turns brings about a peace on earth that has never been seen before. The world has never known such peace, but it is time for peace to reign on earth now. NOW.

There is not one heart on earth which is identical to another. Each and every individual's heart is as a snowflake, different in form from another. The common thread being love. There is not an individual on earth that is incapable of loving. We all have the capacity to love. Once again, there is choice. We choose whether or not we want to love. Why wouldn't someone want to love? This seems like a simple question, yet not so easy to answer for most. It is because people become comfortable in their hate. Can you imagine being comfortable in hating? It is something I can't fathom, but it is nevertheless a reality for some. Terrorists are comfortable hating. Murderers are comfortable hating. The majority of criminals are comfortable hating. Some have family members and neighbors who are comfortable hating. Why? Because most of the people who are involved in this hate grew up being hated, unloved or unwanted, or learned hate from their parents, peers or by those in societies or cultures which condone hatred. They have just turned away from their godly hearts and play into Satan's game. It is the greatest evil on earth and it is alive and well and living in our society and in societies all over the world. It must stop!

In order for the hate to stop, love must prevail. It takes one godly heart to change the world. When you get upset with someone, no matter what the reason, FORGIVE them! No matter who wrongs you, no matter how bad they have made you feel, no matter what the situation, forgive them! It is hard to do if you are not used to doing it, but once you start practicing forgiveness, then the one who is forgiven has been given a blessed gift by you! Man alive! What a great feeling to walk away from someone knowing that you were the better person for having forgiven them. If your pride should get in the way and you cannot find it in your heart to forgive them, then pray about it! Ask God to teach you about letting go of pride and to learn how to forgive. It is perhaps the greatest lesson on earth. When forgiveness is not present, hate abounds. Why harbor hate in your heart when you can feel the joys of forgiveness? If there is a choice, why not choose something that not only makes YOU feel good, but makes the one you are forgiving feel great!

Can you ask for forgiveness? Once again, pride can get in the way. How many times have you found yourself in a pickle, where you have done something wrong and hurt someone terribly and cannot find it in your heart to ask them for forgiveness? I know, it is difficult to ask for forgiveness. One would think that the other person would just walk right over to you and say, "I forgive you, friend!" but it doesn't always work that way. By going up to that person and asking them to forgive you, you allow them the choice to forgive or not to forgive. If they choose to not forgive they are doing themselves a great disservice. For they are telling you that they are going to harbor ill feelings within them regarding the given situation and that is a sad, sad thing. Man alive! You would think all people would want to forgive and forget but it doesn't always work this way. When you have asked someone to forgive you for something and they do not forgive you, know that God has forgiven you and you will receive his blessings for this. Blessings come in all shapes and sizes, so be on the lookout for your blessings from him. They will come in the form of knowledge and growth and they may come in the form of new friends and new, very wonderful experiences. Your friend, on the other hand, will experience things which will keep coming back to haunt them until they finally learn how to forgive. Lessons, lessons and more lessons.

We are human beings and we all deserve to be forgiven for the mistakes that we make. Actually, I do not believe in mistakes, only lessons learned. So remember that when you keep forgiveness in your heart, you are climbing the ladder of spirituality and it is one of the greatest rungs on the ladder.

Finally, learn how to ask for forgiveness even when you feel that you are not responsible for any misgivings. One day, I did something that made a few people very unhappy. Although the thing I was going to do was a very godly thing, they saw it as me stepping on their toes, so they ganged up on me. I received nasty, hateful e-mails from a few people who I thought were my friends. Not only did these people scorn me, they sent these hate letters to quite a few friends in our mutual group of friends and thus spread their hatred all over the place. It broke my heart! I didn't feel as though I had done anything wrong! One of the haters told me that I owed them all an apology. I thought, *Are you kidding me?!* There was no way I was going to apologize to them for not doing anything wrong. So, I sat on this situation for a few days and questioned my own heart about what I should do.

Time went by and eventually, I went up to the person who had really started this whole mess, who was the instigator of this hateful situation, and I told her I wanted to bury the hatchet.

She was stunned and just stood there looking at me and said to me, "All right, but only if you look at me now and apologize."

I did. I looked into her eyes and said, "Please forgive me for hurting you and the others." Then I hugged her and all was well. Needless to say she walked off a little shocked, but I sure felt better knowing that the hatchet had been buried and a load came off my shoulder.

A year or so later, I was at a concert and saw her sitting with a friend in the row in front of me and down a few seats. During the intermission, I called out to her and waved at her. She waved back and when the concert was all over she came up to me and looked me in the eyes and said, "Melanie, now it is my turn." She proceeded to say she was sorry for everything which had transpired and she gave me the biggest bear hug on earth. It was a time of healing and it was a time for new friendships and a big sigh of goodness. Forgiveness is GREAT! MAN ALIVE! Forgiveness is the most wonderful thing ever, if all would just learn about it and not allow stubborn and foolish pride to get in the way.

To love another's heart is to allow forgiveness to reign supreme. To love another's heart is to understand another's heart. Don't be so quick to judge another. You have no idea what that individual has had to deal with their entire life, nor do you know what lies within the deepest realms of that person's heart. Understand others by knowing that you are different from all people, and in turn others are different from you, though you all have the capacity to love. Understanding another's heart means to know that their heart needs to love and be loved. Do everything you can to make other people feel good. Make it a contest for yourself. See how many people you can make smile in the course of a day, a week a month. Make it your goal to always say nice things to strangers. Make it a goal to bring some laughter into a person's soul. Make it a point always to bring out the best you can in others. Make it a focus to put others before yourself. Open car doors for those who have their arms full, open the doors for the elderly and little children. Smile at the checker at the grocery store and tell them how nice they look and what a great smile they have. Ask a teen if they need help with their homework and how they feel about life. Get on a teen's level and appreciate the fact that you were once a teen yourself. Talk with them, not AT them. Believe it or not, the way to a teenager's heart is communication. They just want someone to listen. Ask a young child what they love, what makes them happy, get on your hands and knees and play with them, fly a kite with them, eat a Popsicle with them. Go to the local nursing home and sit and read to the residents there, or share any gift that you possess with them. Call your parents, call your children, call all of your relatives and tell them you love them as often as possible. Send e-cards to your email buddies for no reason at all, in fact, send them cards in the regular mail to let them know you love them and are willing to go to more extensive measures to let them know this. Go to your neighbors' house with a plate full of brownies, just because. Do the same with animals—not feed them brownies, but go to the local animal shelter and spend some time with the animals there; in fact, adopt one! Pay the toll for the car behind you at the toll booth, pay for the meal for the car behind you at your local fast food restaurant. Do everything and all you can for everyone you know and everyone you don't know. You will surely be blessed. Remember that you are the one who will make so many positive changes in the lives of those around you, all the while transforming your life into the most godly life you can ever imagine. God loves you, he loves all people and he needs your help! He needs you to think about him and keep him in your heart and the best way to do this is by keeping everyone around you in your heart. Get rid of all hate, and smile, because what your spirit can do is transform the world! MAN ALIVE!

Mark 11:25—*"And whenever you stand praying, if you have anything against anyone, forgive him, that your Father in heaven may also forgive you your trespasses."*

Matthew 18:21-22—*21 Then Peter came to Jesus and asked, "Lord, how many times shall I forgive my brother when he sins against me? Up to seven times?" 22 Jesus answered, "I tell you, not seven times, but seventy-seven times".*

John 13:34—*"A new commandment I give unto you, That ye love one another; as I have loved you, that ye also love one another."*

Relinquishing Control

How many people do you know who want to control everything around them? How many people have you lived with who try to control you? It is a major dilemma, for those who think they are in control are the ones who are really out of control. By attempting to control all things, we are fooling ourselves. When God created the earth and then created man, he was in control, and he is still in control today. The person who gives up their life to God does not only relinquish control, but is guided by the greatest force in the universe and thus, all things become easier and far less stressful.

When I was nineteen years old, I became a manager for a fast food restaurant. It was a difficult thing for I was not used to being in a position of control. In this case, there needed to be a semblance of authority and control or there would have been mass chaos in this establishment. This kind of control in one's life is necessary. As a leader, a boss, an owner or manager, there must be order, discipline and control. As a parent, it holds true as well. Whenever a person is put into the position of authority, they need to be able to control what is going on around them and thus control the situation and the people who look up to them as authority figures. On earth, in your life, it would be God who is the manager, the boss, the all-knowing figure whom you look up to in order to get things done. When I mention relinquishing control, I mean that you need to realize that there is a being who watches over you, who guides you, who inspires and blesses you, who is ultimately the controller, and we all need to trust in that force. Have you ever worked for a boss who is so controlling that you feel like you have no say-so in anything you do? I think many of us at a time or two in our lives have experienced working with someone like this. In actuality, however, this person is out of control. This boss usually has a high turnover rate of employees, and cannot even control his or her own personal life. Many people who are in positions such as this, who overcompensate their authority by making threats, or are extremely difficult to work with, are usually very insecure people who use bullying tactics to achieve their end results, which usually are not productive. You may have heard the phrase, "You can catch more flies with honey than you can with vinegar." How true this phrase is, and I have seen this in the workplace. I have also seen the former. Those managers and bosses who constantly praise their employees for a job well done and work alongside their employees to help them through their jobs are the ones with the greatest control, as they set an example for others and they also have the lowest turnover rates of employees. The point I am making is that God is the greatest controller of all, the greatest boss, the greatest manager, the greatest being ever. He doesn't expect more than what he knows you are capable of. He is a good trainer, he is fair and just, he will work alongside you, and with you in all ways, he respects you and will never put you down and he will continually praise you for a job well done. More than anything else, he will forgive you when you err, he will forgive you for being human and he knows that you will stumble along the way, yet he will never terminate your employment! He gives chances. If you screw up somewhere along the way, he allows you to learn once again and he does this with the greatest of patience and ease. God is the ultimate controller, for he allows you the freedom of walking the earth and doing your work allowing for mistakes and erring, allowing for your space and your needs. He also gives you choices, and will allow you to make these choices so that you learn from them.

There are a great many people who do not recognize God. He isn't seen as a physical entity, so he is all but forgotten for some. People will rise in the morning from their beds and get themselves ready for work, they will proceed to drive to their jobs and ho-hum themselves to the time clock, then start their work day dreading their boss, dreading their work, dreading their lives. It does not have to be this way! If people would find their spiritual selves and reach out to God to help them through their day, they will find that their lives are controlled by him and that all things will go exactly as planned. Even on the worst of days, there are lessons to learn from them. A bad day at work should be considered a blessing as it is a deitous lesson in patience, perseverance, and fortitude. Never give up! If you are working for someone who is extremely controlling, then try to understand their heart and where they are coming from. Recognize that this person may be totally stressed out because their financial goals have not been met. Many bosses do not mean to take their stress out on their employees, yet so many times it seems this way. They may be having troubles in their personal life as well. It is not easy being a boss for they need to oversee all things, the financial end of things, and how the operation is running overall. Have patience with your boss and say nice things to him or her, ask them for feedback on how you are doing, smile and at least pretend that you like what you are doing! You need not stay in a situation where you are being mistreated, however. If you are totally miserable, then ask God to find you work somewhere else and let him control that path in your life. If you are the boss, remember what it was like to be an employee and do not demand superhuman perfection in anyone. This is unrealistic! Be kind to those who work for you, for without them, you would not be able to run your business. Ask God to help you with your workload and in how to go about gaining the greatest production from your employees and remember that God can do a much better job through you than you can do all by yourself.

It is also important to have some control on the home front. This is crucial. When control is not there, there is no discipline, and when there is no discipline, there is no respect. When there is no respect, there is bitterness and resentment. When there is bitterness and resentment, there is a seed for hate. When there is hate, there is no family. Do you see how it all works hand in hand and how the weed grows? There MUST be control in the home; however, the control need not be a dictatorship! Man alive! I have seen this time and time again on my journey in life. Many parents refuse to allow their children the freedoms that they deserve because the parents fear losing control of the child. If they could realize that there needs to be a letting up of the reins in some cases, so that the child may experience the gift of learning responsibility. When a parent does not grace the child with a reason for his or her yanking back of the reins, then the child is left without an answer, and the answer is important so that the child may learn. When a parent does not grace his child with an answer it also stagnates communication, which is essential in teaching and respecting one another. This is a parent's way of trying to control the child. We hear so often the phrase, "Because I said so!" Well then, I guess we know who is in control, right? Exactly. The parent in this case is telling the child, "I am the one in control and you will abide by my rules!" So the child walks away knowing that the parent is the one in control, but the child also sees this as stubborn, indignant, and unfair. Life isn't always fair, so be it. There is a fine line between disciplining with this type of control and going to extremes to the point where it is very unfair to the child. There is a way to control without being unfair. It is important for the parent to remember what it was like to be a child. So many times, parents turn into their own parents. They find that they are doing to their own child exactly what their parents did to them. Have you ever done this? I know I have. I remember raising my two boys and seeing so much of my mother in myself, who was strict, yet allowed us the freedom to make many of our own choices as teenagers. I respected her a great deal and allowed this to pour through onto my own children. My mother and I had our share of arguments because I couldn't get her to listen to me. She was a single parent raising five teenagers, with a very stressful job. I sometimes felt as though I was burdening her as her reactions to me were not always the gentlest. If I could have just had her listen to what I was saying, but she was very caught up in her control or lack thereof at the time. I saw her go off half cocked sometimes in a tizzy or rage and I believe this was due to financial stress, the stress of raising five children on a limited income, working in the social service field, and so on. Her control on us was mid-range, I believe. She had so much on her plate that I think by the time we were all teenagers she had thrown her hands into the air and said, "Do what you will and hopefully I have done a good enough job molding you over the years that you will make sensible choices and intelligent decisions." Trying to control five teenagers sounds like a stressful job, doesn't it? For her, it was, and also it was a blessing. She was the greatest of mothers and I will always carry a deep and admirable respect for her. Being a parent DOES require control, but let it be God working through you. Ask God to guide you in your parenting, so that all in the family are respectful to each other and grace takes its place in the home.

To relinquish control means to be secure enough in yourself to be able to do so. Being secure means knowing that you will fare just fine because there is a higher being watching out for you. You do not need to run all over the place trying to make everything perfect. You do not need to feel guilt because things are not perfect. You do not need to expect perfection in your children, your siblings, your parents, your friends and even the strangers you meet on the street. You do not need to feel as though your life must be run like clockwork and precise to the minute. You do not need to expect perfection in your employees or your co-workers. Relinquishing control means acceptance. Acceptance of yourself and others and the entire world around you. Knowing also that where there is pain, there is a reason for it being there. Where there is love, there is a reason for it being there. Where there is turmoil and struggle, there is a reason for it also. Only control what is humanly possible and do it in a way which makes others around you grateful for having you there. Do not fear or worry about your life. Once you realize that God is the ultimate controller, your life does not need to be perfect. By controlling all things you are demanding perfection. Perfection only exists in the spirit of God. Be perfect in your spiritual life with God as your guide, and you will not need to fear imperfection. In a simple way, look at life like this. Nature is God. Nature is perfect. You are as a branch on a tree which is all natural. You are to bend, to blow with the wind, to bow down, to rise up, to be fruitful and bear leaves, to branch out and make an impact in the world.

This is being perfect. Your perfection lies in the fact that you exist. You are a part of God and God is a part of you. In that lies perfection. Allow God to help you to relinquish the control that stagnates your growth. Let God be your controller and sway with the wind. Do not force your branch on the other branches in the tree of life or the tree shall ultimately fall and you will bring others down with you. God controls all people who are faithful unto him. We are as the clouds in the sky, and how he can move the clouds is remarkable. We are called upon to be as the grace of the clouds, poised and obedient and allow God to control our movements. Relinquish control and free yourself. Let God control all things in your life and do not worry, for in your faith the Lord will then bring all things unto you.

Job 37:14-16—*14 "Listen to this, Job; stop and consider God's wonders. 15 Do you know how God controls the clouds and makes his lightning flash? 16 Do you know how the clouds hang poised, those wonders of him who is perfect in knowledge?"*

Matthew 6:25-26—*25 "Therefore I say to you, do not worry about your life, what you will eat or what you will drink; nor about your body, what you will put on. Is not life more than food and the body more than clothing? 26 Look at the birds of the air, for they neither sow nor reap nor gather into barns; yet your heavenly Father feeds them. Are you not of more value than they?"*

Gratitude

As your life becomes more and more spiritual, your thankfulness for all things becomes much more pronounced, for you realize that what you have been given in this life is essential in learning lessons on earth and in finding joy. Even the most ordinary and simplest of things become that for which you are grateful. How many people though are grateful for all the terrible things which have happened to them in life? Not many. Most people look upon their past issues and struggles as something horrible and would rather just leave it all in the past and move forward, but there is a reason for everything.

In my own life, I have overcome many a difficult situation. I have learned through my spiritual growth that these things all had to be in order for me to move forward. You cannot move forward in life without experiencing some of the negative which life seems to offer. We can sit back and curse our choices and our circumstances or we can embrace them. If we curse the choices we have made which have led us into difficult situations, and if we curse others because of these situations, we are doing a disservice to ourselves and others. We will not move forward and we cease to learn and grow. If, on the other hand, we look upon these situations as a possibility for growth and spiritual awakening, we can see them as stepping stones which lead us into enlightenment. It is not a bad thing to look back into our pasts and remember how terrible a given situation was, but it is important to learn where these struggles have led us into positive growth.

Forgiveness must remain a priority on our journey though. Sometimes, we look at the situations which have caused us much pain and want to blame others for these difficult times. We refuse to see where we, ourselves, have been part of the problem and thus, we carry in our hearts a bitterness not only to the given circumstance, but a bitterness towards others. There is not one situation in life which we cannot learn from. All situations are there for our learning. In our spiritual growth, we ask God to make us more aware of the lessons that he is teaching us. But it is very important for us to make the choice to want to learn. What I see all the time is a multitude of people walking around sorrowful, vengeful, hateful and distressed at their situations, without giving thought as to why things are the way they are. Instead of listening to their hearts as to why things are the way they are, they walk around grumbling and fussing as to how they have been wronged, or how awful their lives seem to be. Taking no responsibility for their choices, and leaving little consideration for what their lessons are. Once lessons are realized, the thoughts become ever godly, and a forgiveness for the given situations prevails, then it all becomes so clear. It doesn't mean that people just forget about what has transpired or what is presently transpiring, it means they can make their way through it with ease and clear insight. I like to view our lives as a journey, walking fervently through a dark forest, having God there to help us through this forest. There are going to be rocks in the road, and things that reach out to us and smack us right in the face, but with the light of God there to cling to and to hold on to, we know that we will get down the path gracefully. When God is ever present during not only the times where the path seems to be well lit, but during the times that seem the darkest, then there is a light that guides which lives within. When walking through the forest without God, the path remains dark and it becomes ever more difficult to make it through on this journey. When we hit the difficult and darkest times on this path, there is no light shining and we will fall, we will hurt ourselves, we will curse all in our way and remain blinded. It is not until we accept God on this journey that the path seems more open, without as many stones to step over, and the light at the end of the road is there waiting for us. God is our flashlight and the batteries never die. Without this flashlight, we are blindfolded and bound to the darkest forest ever. As our light shines brighter, we are able to see so much more around this path we travel, and thus become more grateful to the things which we can see all around us. Even during the difficult times, we are aware of the good around us and these good things enable us to ford on ever strong. Because of the light that is ever present, we are able to see beauty on our journey and become so thankful for this glorious life we are living.

Being grateful does not mean to just be grateful for the good that comes your way. It means to be grateful for all the bad things as well. People miss the boat on this a lot. Why would anyone be grateful for bad things that happen in their lives? Because these bad things teach about good things. People have asked me why God would allow so many to be killed in the tsunami that took place in Sri Lanka and surrounding islands. I have been asked about Hurricane Katrina and the tragedy at Columbine High School. Why would God allow these things to happen? I would tell them to search their hearts. I would explain to them that God takes people home to heaven in a situation like this, to teach people that there is a heaven and that he will sacrifice lives to teach others about compassion, and how to come together in their hearts. In all disasters we are called upon to come to the aid of others, to embrace those left behind and to teach them about faith. When people die it is not a bad thing, for we will all be joined together in heaven. It is very difficult for those family members and friends left behind. They will grieve and they will question why. God does not want us to mourn for long. It is important for those in situations like this to remember that heaven is only a prayer away and that their loved ones will always be with them in spirit. Their loved ones will also be with them in heaven when they return home to God. Sure, it is easy for me to say this, because I didn't have a loved one who died in any tragic disaster, but I have had loved ones die in other ways. We are asked by God to rejoice in their leaving the earth for there is life waiting after this life. To be grateful means to be understanding about this and to be very thankful that God has taken those whom we love home to a place where life continues and it's peaceful and full of bliss. It does not mean we will be happy and joyous about their physical presence leaving us, but then we are thinking only of ourselves and our own loss. We are called upon to remember that this life is like the blink of an eye in perspective and we will be joined with those we love in heaven when we are also called home to this wonderful place. It doesn't mean we won't miss our loved ones, it means that we are to remember that there is life after life on earth for those who keep God in their hearts.

We may not always know why bad things happen to us until long after they happen to us. We do not always understand why a given situation befalls us. The answers sometimes become clear long after the situation has transpired. For example, there was a time in my life that I remember vividly. It was the worst time in my life that I can recall. I was getting a divorce and was losing everything. My marriage, my home, my childcare business and more. The following week, I found myself alone in a house where there used to be jovial voices all around. I had been running a childcare business out of my home for seven years at that point. I knew I would not be able to keep the house, for my childcare business would not supply the income needed for the cost of living expenses. I knew I would have to sell the house and quit the business I was running. Never before had I been in such a position. I lost it all. I fell into such a deep depression and just laid my head on the kitchen table and cried until I could cry no more. I asked God why. Why would he do this to me? I had been a good person my entire life and been good to others. I had been forgiving of others and giving as well. I just could not understand why something like this would happen to me! I was mad at God. Or at least I thought I was. The truth is, I was mad at the situation and I wanted to blame God for it. I knew that all things happened for a reason and there was a lesson in all of this, but I just couldn't find the answer. It was as if the flashlight had been turned off in this very dark forest. What was I going to do? Where would I go? It was that evening that I realized if I let go of God at that point, I would surely be walking without a flashlight and the road would be very dark ahead. But I wanted to be mad at him. This is what I mean by the very difficult situations that seem to befall us, that come to us when it is not because of our own choice. It was not my choice to get a divorce and it was not my choice that I would have to sell the house, it was inevitable. Life can be very puzzling! So, why was all of this happening? I had to sit there and cry for a while and allow the grief to take place. This is important. To not keep these feelings inside. Once I was all cried out, I could rationally think about where to turn next. Do I ditch God in my anger? For a few minutes I really wanted to. I was so angry with him for putting me in this situation. I am sure many of you can relate. When you have everything you have ever loved taken from you and your life is turned upside down, what you want to do is lash out at the forces that be. I screamed out, "Why are you doing this to me!?" Do you think that I found this out right away? No. There wasn't a light bulb that turned on instantly, but there was a feeling of *this has to be in order for other things to come*. I didn't know what was lying down the road, it was too dark at that point, but it was vital that I keep this flashlight turned on. In other words, it was crucial that I keep God alive and well in my heart so that he would shine on the road that I would travel. I needed to climb out of that dark pit that I had fallen into and I would do it with God's help, his strength, his light. The next morning, I called a friend who lived in a city on the Western Slope in Colorado and asked if this friend had any place in his home where I could stay until I could get back on my feet. Amazingly enough, he had a basement with a bedroom in it and places for all my things to be stored. He had just gotten a divorce and said he could use the company. He didn't even charge me rent! I moved away and started to heal. I worked on his landscape and made an angel garden with lots of wildflowers, bushes, and a pathway made of bark, logs of wood and stone to line the pathway. With the money I received in equity for the sale of my home, I was able to help my friend with his house by buying him new carpet, linoleum for his kitchen floor and a new refrigerator. All in all, it was the best of all situations at the time. I was able to give back to someone who was helping me out. I could have cared less about giving away a lot of my money because by helping him out, he was helping me out and I didn't even consider it losing money, but money well spent. I found a job in this little town taking care of developmentally disabled folks, and soon had so many new friends that were like angels sent down from heaven! The job allowed me to travel all over the area, driving around the disabled clients to see the beauty of the Western Slope of Colorado, and I was getting paid for this! Man alive! It was perhaps one of the best jobs I had ever worked and a blessing for me as I learned a great deal about developmentally disabled people. In the meantime, I had gotten over the loss of my marriage, realizing that it was really no loss at all, as our marriage was not what it should have been and I had been living in denial for such a long time. I remained in contact with the rest of my family over the phone and through letters. I had a place to live and even though it was the basement of someone else's home, it was cozy and perfect for me. I had a job that was a blessing and all seemed to heal just fine. My life has moved on from that point as well and I continue to be led along such an illuminated path. When I look back on that time when I was laying my head on the table, crying my heart out to God, I can still remember the pain of loss. It was perhaps the worst time of my life, but had it not happened, I would not have been blessed with the many new friends I have met in the years since, nor would I have been blessed with so many wonderful experiences. I also would never have met the current man in my life, who fills my world with so much joy and happiness. I never realized at that dreaded time, crying at my kitchen table with my head down in sorrow, that life would have been so good to me. At the same time, something in me did know. I knew that I needed God more at that time than ever for it is in the most difficult times we must cling to our faith, our hope and our light. For all bad situations, there is a godly result waiting. We must be grateful for all things. For the water that runs from our taps, for the earth in which we walk, for the wild things that live and breathe all around us. We must be grateful for the clothes on our backs, the food which we eat, the farmers who toil so that we can eat, the people all around us in all service fields who help us maintain our lifestyles. We must be grateful for the smallest of things and the largest of things, but most of all, we must find gratitude for the things about which we feel worst, because in those things we learn to cling to our hope and our faith and our belief that God is always with us. For all which seems negative, there is a positive waiting. It may take some time to realize what the positive is, what the lesson is that we are supposed to learn, but it all comes to those who keep the light on. Had I not experienced such a loss in my life, I never would have realized the gifts I have received since. Do not despair, for even in the darkest of all situations, God is there, shining his light in your heart. Just keep the flashlight on at all times and you will never stray long in the darkness. Be grateful for all things and tell God so.

John 8:12—*Then Jesus spoke to them again, saying, "I am the light of the world. He who follows Me shall not walk in darkness, but have the light of life."*

Giving and Receiving

Who is the giver if there is none to receive? Who also is the receiver should they not be given unto?

Giving and receiving go hand in hand, you cannot have one without the other. Most people will tell you that they love to give. Yet, who doesn't love to receive as well? Let's be honest. Who wouldn't love to see their husband come home at night with a dozen red roses in his arms as he walks through the door? Who doesn't love to receive an e-mail card from a friend, just because? Who doesn't love to receive gifts in regular mail, especially when it is unexpected? There isn't a one of us out there in this big world who doesn't love to receive, whether it is a physical gift or a hug and kiss, or just a smile from someone else, which should also be considered a blessed gift. A smile could very well be one of the greatest gifts on earth.

For the longest time in my life, I was a giver. Sure, I would receive gifts and relished in the opening of them, but the pleasure that I received from giving was the ultimate. To see someone jumping up and down for joy because of a gift I had given was such a blessed thing! When I would see the look on the recipient's face, it did something to my heart that was unmatchable. Giving was glorious, and I did it often. Every chance that I could. I would not always give monetary gifts as

I hadn't the resources to do so, but even a card in the mail was something I would consider. My mother was one such recipient of my giving. I remember that long after I had moved out of the house, I would drive thirty minutes to her house early in the morning on a Saturday and before she would wake, would have her entire house cleaned and her coffee made. Why? Because I knew she would be elated and knew also that it would save her precious time on the weekend as she worked hard during the week. My mother also knew that I was a giver from very early on. I am wary of boasting here as I do not intend to convey this, I only want to convey the feelings of what it is like to be a giver in a world where we need much giving. I was cautioned by my mother early on about my giving as she was concerned about my being taken advantage of as I gave so freely. She didn't want me to get hurt. It was hard for me to say no to anyone. As I grew older, I found that her concerns were warranted as time and time again, I was taken advantage of. However, I eventually learned to give in moderation instead of giving to a point where I was used and abused for it. It had gotten to the point where I was all giver and found it very difficult to receive. I spent so much time giving of myself that when someone gave to me, I didn't know quite how to respond. It got to the point that I would tell the person giving to me, "You shouldn't have done that!" Quite the wrong thing to say to someone giving, but live and learn. In order to be a good giver, one must learn how to receive.

In my forties, I was really taught about how to receive. Shortly after the divorce, I found myself in unfamiliar territory. I had lost everything—my home, my job and my security. At this point in my life I had to call upon friends for help emotionally and physically. It was very difficult for me to be on the receiving end for a change. As any giver knows, it is one thing to give freely and another to be the recipient of another's generosity. I found myself not knowing how to thank those who had supported me and given so generously. I didn't have the money to pay them for that which they had given so freely, and I didn't have the words. There I was, stuttering the words "thank you" and "you didn't have to." In response, my friends would tell me that I had given to them and this was their way of helping me out now. Did I ever feel uncomfortable! Why? Because I was not usually the one on the receiving end. I just didn't know how to receive and do it well. It was time to learn. At this strange time in my life, I became friends with a group of people with a similar bond. We shared the same love for a certain celebrity who had died a year or so earlier. His following was tremendous. We would all get together and remember him through song, and gatherings. During my divorce, these friends pulled together and supported me tremendously. I started receiving wonderful cards and gifts in the mail. Yet, I felt as though I should be reciprocating as to share the giving. It was difficult to just accept and thank without giving anything in return. My thoughts were, *Hmmmm, I should be giving back to my friends, yet I don't know what to give back for all the things given to me.* Dilemma. Would I lose friends because I didn't send anything to them? I haven't yet. There would be letters of thanks I would send to them, explaining to them that I had nothing to give as I didn't have the money to buy them anything, not even a card at that point. I was apologizing for my lack of giving, but that was all I had ever known for a great many years. What I was missing was learning how to be a good receiver. The gracious giver is the one who gives unconditionally, without expecting anything in return, and the gracious receiver is one who understands that the gift was unconditional. None of my friends expected anything from me. Shock! Nobody expected anything from me! I learned that my true friends were givers too and gave to me out of the love they felt and that was enough. I would pray for God to bless me with some money so that I could give back to them, but money was scarce and what little money I did make, I needed to keep for myself in order to live. He was teaching me. I didn't even have enough money for the cards I used to buy for friends. It scared me. Realizing that my previous income used to allow for my giving, the income I currently took in did not allow for this. Man alive! How was I going to give to my friends? Reality-check time. I decided to give in other ways. I just had to change my means of giving by being there for my friends emotionally and in any other way I could dream up. I would write songs and poetry for them, utilizing my creative gifts. Some very good friends of mine asked me to hold an online church service on Sunday mornings and so I did this and I realized that was another way I could give back. Eventually, I came to realize that I feared losing friends because of what I could not give, instead of realizing that giving was not a prerequisite for my friendships. The best thing a person can give of oneself is exactly that. Oneself. I also realized that receiving gifts and support from friends is precious but the greatest gift that they could possibly give me was their love and support. Finally, pressures eased up and I came to understand that this had all been a very important lesson in my life. Giving and receiving.

It is not fair to the giver to not be a great receiver in return, and vice versa. One cannot be without the other. It is best to be gracious upon receiving by thanking the giver honestly and sincerely. This makes the giver feel blessed in the heart. On the other hand, the giver must not expect too much from the receiver. One should not give to expect something back, it should be done unconditionally. A mere thank you should suffice, all the while knowing that God sees what you give and in that, your blessings will come back threefold. Also, the amount spent on a gift should not even be considered as greater than the smallest gift given. God does not see the difference between giving a friend a beautiful card with heartfelt thoughts and a brand-new red Ferrari. Giving from the heart knows no measure. One should not measure friendships and love by the size of a gift, for God knows the heartfelt sincerity which goes into the thought of giving.

There was a time that I ventured out to the mailbox and reached in to receive what I figured would be bills. I looked into my stack of envelopes and there was a card from a friend I had met in a group I was involved in. This girl and I had met at a gathering in Aspen. We knew each other but had never had the fortunate pleasure to do much together. Out of the blue she sent me a card that touched my heart. There were handwritten words from her, telling me how much I meant to her and how I had touched her life. Man alive! I had no idea she felt that close to me. I had never expected such a card and I saved it, and look upon it from time to time. I have a little file in my file cabinet labeled *Miracles*. There her card sits, and whenever I am feeling a bit down or need a lift, I take out her card and read it. Small gift? I don't think so. Big gift...truly. The thing is, value is unimportant, the heart knows no difference in the value of a gift in a monetary sense. The truest and godliest of hearts do not place any emphasis on one gift over another. The greatest gift of all is the gift of love and love comes in many ways. Love comes in many shapes and sizes. But love is still love no matter the size, no matter the quantity, no matter the monetary value, no matter what. Do not place value on the gift given, place the value on the heart of the giver. Love all you receive but love the giver most of all. What is it to receive a dandelion from a grandchild in comparison to a rose from your lover? You cannot compare, for love is love, through and through.

Be a sincere giver, but at the same time, be a gracious receiver, for one without the other is like the sun without the moon.

Luke 14:12-14—*Then Jesus said to his host, "When you give a luncheon or dinner, do not invite your friends, your brothers or relatives, or your rich neighbors; if you do, they may invite you back and so you will be repaid. But when you give a banquet, invite the poor, the crippled, the lame, the blind, and you will be blessed. Although they cannot repay you, you will be repaid at the resurrection of the righteous."*

Loving Your Enemies

This is perhaps the most difficult of all lessons to learn on earth. How can we be expected to love our enemies? What does it mean to love an enemy?

In a perfect world, there would be no such thing. We do not live in a perfect world, however, and there will be hate on earth until the day that people realize that it just doesn't work. When Jesus was on earth, he spoke to people about loving their enemies for he realized that there would be wars, disputes and turmoil among the masses. Even during the time that he walked the earth, there were wars going on and hate infiltrating into the smallest of towns. As sad as it is to realize, it is running rampant in our world today. Why? Good question. Surely there would be peace on earth should we see an end to hate. Peace can be realized only if there is a conscientious effort on the parts of all people, but it can start with one. Let's start with you.

Take some time this week and focus on your feelings toward others as you head into your job, into the grocery store, or anywhere else you may need to go. Focus on your feelings toward the people around you. If there is one negative feeling toward anyone, write it down. Get it out of your system. It may be the person who cut you off while driving or was tailgating you on the way to your destination. It may be the person who cut in line at the bank, or the person who bumped their cart into yours at the store, or the person who took too long in front of you at the gas pump. It may be the preschool teacher who didn't pay enough attention to your child, or your childcare provider who gave you a bad report on your child for the day. It could be the family that lives next door, or the group of people living in the seedy side of town, the man who held up the convenience store down the street, and all the other criminals who are causing much havoc in your neighborhood. You might feel total disgust for those people you see on your news channel at night, the ones who are responsible for so much crime. It might even be a family member or a friend who has hurt you, or perhaps you hurt them and they are unforgiving. All negative thought and feeling breeds more negative thought and feeling. We are conditioned throughout our entire lives to get angry with others. Our own children have heard our negative words regarding others that we spew out so freely. We may not realize it, but our children take this with them and, in turn, act upon what we have unconsciously taught them. It is not as though we are totally aware of what we are doing when we get angry. For some reason, we lose our sanity when we go off the deep end. Our children, however, pick up on it all and thus repeat our actions in their own lives. When they are grown, their own children will see this as well and will act on it. To be loving, peaceful and forgiving of all others takes an effort which requires a great deal of prayer and focus. Especially when one has known no other way. How easy it is to get angry! How easy it is to hate! Man alive! So easy, in fact, that it feels good sometimes to just let loose on someone! The adrenaline rush is amazing! It also seems that we feel so much better after we have taken our frustration out on someone else. What we are doing is watering the hate weed that still thrives within us. The weed must be pulled. Hateful words are the biggest weed of all. It is our words that will destroy and it seems that our world is filled with people spilling out hateful words towards others all the time. We hear it, see it and we become privy to it, lest we turn away, we become a big part of it all. We see this at sporting events, where people are supposed to go and have a nice time. We see this during political campaigns. If things don't work out the way we want, we get upset and words are thrown about as if other people's feelings don't matter. We use the word "HATE" so freely that it has become part of our everyday vocabulary. I am guilty of this, everyone is guilty of this. I caught myself just the other day telling my boyfriend how much I hate lima beans. Well, that doesn't hurt anyone, but I am still using the word and it is still living there in my vocabulary and it is time to say so long to hate once and for all. A better way of phrasing would be to say, "I have never liked lima beans." It is time for people to become consciously aware of the words they are using, even if they are used in a lighter context. Try letting go of the word "hate." It isn't easy, because we have grown up using it.

As you go about your week, jot down the times you got angry with someone, write down how that person made you feel and what you did to overcome the feeling. The more you focus on this, the more aware you become in being able to release the negative in a positive way. How do you release in a positive way? By praying for the person or persons who have done you wrong. This is very hard for some people to do, especially those who are not used to praying much to begin with. If your boss at work upsets you and you detest working with him or her, pray for them and for yourself. Ask God to work in his or her life to bring about their spiritual side in the workplace. Ask God to help you release these negative feelings and he will, you just need to trust that he will.

I am going to touch now on a subject which is very sensitive. This subject pertains to the matter of terrorism. No doubt terrorism is the epitome of hate. When the towers of the World Trade Center fell, the entire world watched in total awe as the towers plummeted to the ground and the loss of life was catastrophic. Families were devastated and the pain unbearable. As I watched this transpire and heard words from people regarding the terrorists and this attack, I was reminded by God that our country has had terrorism weeding its way throughout for a very long time. The terrorism is in our schools, it is in the hearts of our children, bringing to mind the Columbine School tragedy. We have terrorism all around us and have had since I can remember. Rape is an act of terrorism, as is racism, and any act of crime. The 9/11 tragedy was a wake-up call to the fact that terrorism is alive and well and feeding on its own hate. When we hate those who wrong us or our families and friends, we are in essence feeding into the hate, which in turn brings about a strength for terrorism itself. Our country at this very moment is involved in "The War Against Terrorism." This has puzzled me, for isn't war the same thing as terrorism? You cannot fight terrorism, for fighting is what terrorism wants. It is evil, and to wage war on it feeds into it. It doesn't make much sense. We kill, and thus we are killed. We are killed and thus we kill. Many innocent people have lost their lives, not only in the falling of the towers, but in the war that has ensued because of it. When will it end? It won't. Not until people come to realize that war begets war. Hate begets hate. Am I sitting here telling those who lost loved ones in this heinous terrorism act to sit back and forgive the ones who brought it all on? How can I do that gracefully? Had I lost a loved one to the 9/11 incident, I would most assuredly be angry and want to hate those who committed this horrific crime. But in the end, what good would prevail if I did? I would be harboring hatred and thus watering the weed. There needs to be an understanding of where the hate comes from. Those who were involved in this terrorist attack actually believed they were doing something godly. In their minds and hearts this is what they believed, that they would be martyred in heaven by doing so. This is IGNORANCE! Of course everyone wants to hate these people! In their ignorance they are extremely spiritually misguided. If we want this to stop, there must be prayer! Prayer for the coming of Jesus, prayer for the coming of love, prayer for the coming of truth, prayer for the coming of all good and godly things on earth. God is the love, the light and the power of freedom in all that is good! How can we educate our enemies? By showing them the light of God. How? By praying for them, by understanding that their spiritual levels are not where they should or could be, by loving those who harbor hell in their hearts. Yes, I am asking all those who have suffered from this tragedy to pray for those who have done them and their families a significant injustice. This is what Jesus meant by loving your enemies. If Jesus was walking the earth today, I feel he would say the same thing. Had Jesus been here on earth during this tragic event, I am certain that he would have been shaking his head with tears in his eyes that such a thing could have ever taken place, and he would have told us all to reach into our hearts and find forgiveness even for those who have taken the lives of their loved ones. God takes his good and godly children home to heaven. Instantly. Such a blessed thing this is. So many times it is when we least expect it, and a loved one will pass on into a world of bliss where suffering is naught, where peace reigns, where they will meet us again. So hard for people to forgive such a heinous crime, however.

Anger differs from hate. There is what I refer to as righteous anger. Even Jesus was angry when God's temple in Jerusalem was used for merchants selling their wares. It had been turned into a marketplace instead of a place of worship. Jesus got angry but he did not hate. He turned tables upside down and shouted out at the merchants for what they were doing. This did not mean, however, that Jesus hated these people, but he was angry with them. God gets angry! I am certain that he is angry with the terrorists.

Hate. It kills. It takes away. It runs rampant through the veins of the spiritually ignorant. You are better than this! To live a spiritual life is to have faith in the life that comes after this one. To know that you will not be separated from your loved ones for long, for this life is as the blink of an eye. To have faith means to love all people for all reasons. To have faith means to pray for those who do not understand about God, Jesus and life and love everlasting. Loving means forgiving and praying for those who do not know what spirituality is all about. It means to pray for the ignorant. It means to accept the fact that we are all human beings sent down to earth to learn all that we can about God and our spiritual hearts. Learning, growing, loving, forgiving, it is all intertwined. It doesn't do anyone any good to harbor hate for anyone! To rise up against hate by hating is foolish! To rise up against hate with love is a blessing. Set the example! The next time someone treats you with hate, turn to them and ask them to slap your other cheek as well. The next time someone tries to steal the shirt off your back, hand them your coat as well. Do not give in to hate by hating in return. Love your enemies by praying for them. Love your enemies by understanding that their hearts are ignorant and must be taught. Love your enemies by looking them in the eye and telling them you love them. Watch the hate melt away. It is like water on the Wicked Witch of the West. By loving those who harbor hate in their hearts, you are killing off their ungodly spirits with the most divine instrument ever given, your own deitous and glorious heart.

Yes, your very own heart, for it is in that heart where God dwells and this is what he would want you to do. Let us all do what God wants for a change instead of what the evil side would want us to do. Love. Turn the hate into love and watch the miracles that ensue.

Now, focus on your feelings the entire week, and then the next week. Turn your negative feelings into positive ones. Instead of hating another human being, ask God to help you pray for that person. Smile at them, forgive them and be understanding for they may not know as much as you do spiritually. You can teach them more about themselves through your own loving actions than they will learn in perhaps a lifetime from others who hate as they might. Love your enemies and allow peace to take its place in the world.

Matthew 5:43-48—*43 "You have heard that it was said, 'Love your neighbor and hate your enemy.' 44But I tell you: Love your enemies and pray for those who persecute you, 45that you may be sons of your Father in heaven. He causes his sun to rise on the evil and the good, and sends rain on the righteous and the unrighteous. 46If you love those who love you, what reward will you get? Are not even the tax collectors doing that? 47And if you greet only your brothers, what are you doing more than others? Do not even pagans do that? 48Be perfect, therefore, as your heavenly Father is perfect."*

Patience

How many times have you been told you have to wait? After a job interview, you have to wait for the prospective employer to call you. When you order a product through the mail, you must wait for it to come. When you call companies on the phone for information you more than likely have been put on hold, and sometimes can't even get a real person's voice. It seems you have been waiting for things your entire life. Waiting for true love to come your way, waiting for the right job, waiting in traffic and in sales lines. Waiting in the grocery store, at the bank, at the gas station. It seems to me that the world is getting tired of waiting. This is where the gift of patience comes in handy. But how does one acquire this special gift? By practicing it, and this is a lot easier when your spiritual self takes hold. There is no such thing as getting anything quickly, at least not the things we want so badly we can taste it.

Patience is not just an acquired skill, it is a blessed gift. It has more to do with one's own mentality than just being able to wait for things. It takes a great deal of patience to run a childcare. It requires extreme patience to work in the people service field, for the temper seems to just want to take over when dealing with other people. To work in any job requires patience. Just when you think you have things under control, a little slip-up and then it all goes haywire and patience has fallen by the wayside. The greatest test of patience comes from being a parent. Children don't mean to be bad, they just sometimes do bad things. They are learning and to be a great parent means to be very understanding and very, very patient. While raising my own two boys, who were as different as night is from day, I would be faced with their squabbling and fighting on a daily basis. It was all I could do to keep my temper in check and under wraps. Occasionally, I would lose it and say things to the boys that were not always the nicest. There we go again, the word issue. It is so vitally important to not let your mouth get the best of you when dealing with your children, for they soak these words up like a sponge. Words hurt. When patience has taken a hiatus the words come and cut like a knife. Words leave scars.

Just when I thought I could be the spokesperson for the patience campaign, having learned it well and put it to so many good uses, I received a jolting setback. I am a songwriter and singer, so I bought myself a very nice sixteen-track recording system and also a keyboard to go along with it. Tired of spending so much money on recording studios, I got the notion that I could record my own songs, arrange them and throw in the strings and flute sounds that I wanted. Little did I know that reading the manual on the mixer/arranger would be like reading legal jargon from an attorney. It had to be translated, number one, and number two, I realized that to do all of this myself would take many different retakes on the recording end. Just the other night I was in my recording studio trying to lay the tracks down for a song I had written. For some reason, I thought I could do this with one take, NOT! After about ten takes, I started getting very upset. My hands started hurting and fingers started aching. I wanted to get it right and I was not about to give up. Two hours passed and I still didn't have the guitar track down. I wanted to cry because at this point, I thought I would never get it down. It was not just that the guitar part hadn't been laid yet, but I had other parts that I needed to get recorded as well, the vocals and the strings and flute parts. I wanted it done and I wanted it done now! Too bad for me, huh? I still don't have that guitar part down! I picked up the guitar the next day and tried again, to no avail. I would get halfway through the song and one of my strings would twang and that would be the end of it, back to square one. At the point of tears, I just put the guitar down in a very disgusted way and said out loud, "Fine, I just won't record that stupid song!" and I left the room in total frustration and anger. As I sat on the couch moping about this, I realized that perhaps I was being taught a lesson in patience here; after all, nothing great has ever been completely created in a matter of just minutes. I thought about Michelangelo, DaVinci, and so many other great artists who worked very hard on their craft which may have taken them years to perfect. Sometimes, we just want things to happen in our time and this is futile thinking. Determination, along with perseverance and patience, is key.

God wants us to be patient, for in HIS time all things happen perfectly. This is true with prayer and I really want to touch on this, for many people believe that their prayers are going unanswered because they haven't been answered their way or in their time. God hears all prayers. He answers all prayers, just maybe not in the way we would like him to. He is the expert in all of this, however, not us. Just because we may run out of patience in our dreaming for things and our praying for things doesn't mean they are not going to happen. For example, I have been writing songs for over thirty years now. To my credit, I have written approximately 110 songs. Over the years, I have sent them out to many recording companies, and to different publishers. To my dismay, they would send the songs back with a kind "No thank you, we are not accepting new submissions at this time." And so on and so on. I received many a rejection. Did it stop me from writing? No. Did it stop me from praying about my dream of becoming a professional songwriter? No. A long time ago, when I had just started writing, singing and playing my twelve-string guitar, I realized that God may have other plans for me. After the songs were sent out and sent back to me, I realized that there must be a very good reason for this, for the songs are not half bad! Perhaps the market is not quite right for my songs, perhaps the radio stations do not think they are quite country enough, or easy listening enough, whatever. My voice may not be well trained enough. There could be many reasons for this dream to have been held back, but I am not giving up! It requires a great deal of patience to realize one's dreams. Perhaps God will decide to use my songs when I am sixty years old. So be it. Perhaps he may never use my songs, but it doesn't matter, because what it boils down to is patience and faith. If the songs never get out into the world, he has given me the gift of being able to compose lyrics, use my ear for the melodies, the talent to play a guitar and a voice to sing. If it means the songwriting is to be used for my own personal enjoyment, then it is fine. But that doesn't mean I am going to give up.

Dreaming is something all people do, letting go of dreams is something that should never be done, for if not for the dreamer we would not have much in the way of the arts, the healing professions, science and so on. I see a great many successful people who never realized their dreams until they were in their golden years. Some people don't realize their dreams until they are no longer here on earth! Man alive! Patience is key, for without it, dreams are blown into the wind and the healthy, persevering spirit dies.

Patience is crucial in the workplace. There is not a one of us who hasn't lost their patience while working. Whether your boss is giving you grief and you get fed up with him/her, or the people alongside whom you are working, or your customers, there will be a time when your patience is tried to the extreme. The lack of patience has been known to cause many a fallout at work. People have lost their jobs and many have lost their families over their lack of patience. It is very important to be patient with others, for there isn't a soul on earth who doesn't err a time or two. Patience requires letting go of stubborn pride. Many who lose their patience become violent and physically hurt, not only material things but people as well. It is a basis for domestic violence and needs to be addressed! The lack of patience destroys!

To exercise patience requires fervent prayer, especially if you are the type of person who flies off the handle very easily. It can be overcome! If you are caught up in a difficult situation where it seems there is no control, then take a deep breath, say a prayer and ask God to work quickly in your heart so that you can easily overcome the turmoil. Patience requires turning away from the anger in your heart and replacing it with positive thought. Easier said than done, I know, but it can become easier as you place your focus on relaxing more, meditating more, breathing deeply and praying. No matter how bad the day has been or is going for you, it can be turned around with prayer and faith. With these two ingredients, you are well on your way to baking the cake of patience. How things turn out will amaze you. When patience is exercised in all situations, the outcome is always more fruitful and beautifully complete. Pray for patience and let it be your gift, so that you will more fully enjoy those around you and also find yourself breathing a lot easier regarding all things. With patience, your dreams will become a reality.

Ecclesiastes 7:8-9—*8 The end of a matter is better than its beginning, and patience is better than pride. 9 Do not be quickly provoked in your spirit, for anger resides in the lap of fools.*

Isaiah 40:31—*But they that wait upon the LORD shall renew their strength; they shall mount up with wings as eagles; they shall run, and not be weary; and they shall walk, and not faint.*

Grace

Grace and patience go hand in hand. You cannot have one without the other. God's grace is perfect in all ways. When we ask God to lead us into our lives with his grace, it is done perfectly. Even when our own lives seem so imperfect, with grace it can be smooth as a feather on the breeze. You have seen figure skaters on television. They float over the ice with the greatest of ease, in fluid movements, and they do this on the thinnest of blades. This is grace. Imagine our lives being just like that! They can be, but it takes prayer and it takes patience when handling the most difficult of situations.

There is a dirt road that I must travel to get to my home in the mountains of Colorado. It is filled with washboard-like bumps that are very hard on my vehicle and the rocks in the road are ever present. I dread traveling down this road but it must be done, so I pray for patience and grace each time I get in my car to make my journey. Life is like this, bumpy and rocky. Let me give you an example of life without grace. I am going to use a woman whom I will call Jane. Jane is a medical assistant who is recently divorced and has three children, a fifteen-year-old son, a seven-year-old son and a three-year-old daughter. Here is Jane's day, without grace.

Jane forgets to set her alarm clock and needs to be at work by 8:00 a.m. Jane has a little over an hour to get to work and also to get her three-year-old to the childcare and her sons off to school. Jane has had a lot on her mind over the past couple of weeks as her child support check has not come, her mother was recently diagnosed with breast cancer and she needs new brakes for her car. Needless to say, Jane has much on her plate and this day has started off all wrong. Jane jumps out of bed, stubs her toe on the bedpost, jumps in the shower and is out of soap. Jane steps out of the shower to get some soap, nearly slips by the sink because of her wet feet, and grabs hold of the sink counter, which twists her wrist. Jane is livid! She finishes her shower and proceeds to get dressed while popping a button off her blouse. She changes blouses and yells to the kids to wake up. Her fifteen-year-old son was up late doing his homework and can't seem to rise and shine. Jane does not have time for coffee this morning and is in a frenzy. Her seven-year-old is dressed and asks his mother for his lunch money, which Jane does not have. She screams for him to make his own lunch so he gets out the peanut butter and jelly, spilling the jelly all over the counter. The three-year-old is being tended to by Jane and she puts her into a high chair with her sippy cup filled with milk. Meanwhile, the fifteen-year-old is slowly rising and coming to the breakfast table sleepy eyed. Jane doesn't have time for her own breakfast so she throws a breakfast bar into her purse. The fifteen-year-old asks Jane if he can borrow the car tonight as he and his friends want to go to a football game. Jane, in total disgust, tells her son absolutely not, and reminds him that he only has his permit and that he must be a stupid idiot for asking such a question. The room is filled with dread. The seven-year-old is walking around on pins and needles as to not upset his mother. The three-year-old is crying because her sippy cup fell off the high chair and milk is splattered everywhere. Jane is cleaning up the milk and tells the fifteen-year-old to go and start the car for her, but he can't find the keys. Everyone starts rummaging around for the keys. After fifteen minutes of frantic searching, the seven-year-old finds the keys in the basement on the end table near the couch. Instead of praising her seven-year-old for finding them, she tells him to clean his mess up on the counter and to get into the car. Just when everyone is securely fastened in their seats, Jane realizes that she left the diaper bag on the kitchen table. She tells her seven-year-old to run in and get it for her and meanwhile, the fifteen-year-old forgot his homework in his room, so he heads out of the car as well. Jane breaks a nail while trying to open the glove box to get out a Kleenex for her runny nose, and meanwhile the three-year-old is crying in the backseat because she doesn't want to go to childcare. Jane has lost it! Everyone gets back into the car and the seven-year-old is quiet as can be, thinking that he must be to blame for all the chaos. Yet, he was the one to make his own lunch, find his mom's keys, help his sister get in her car seat and run in to grab the diaper bag. The seven-year-old is the hero for the day, the peacemaker. Jane is not at peace though. She drives like a maniac, almost wiping out two other cars on the way to the childcare. She hands her daughter to the childcare provider while the child is screaming at the top of her lungs. She runs back to the car and trips while trying to grab the diaper bag out of the backseat. By this time she is spewing out all matter of horrific words, which her children hear. Jane drops the kids off at school, all the while telling them about the chores they must do upon getting home from school, which really sets the kids off. They slam the doors to the car and make their way into the school, where they don't pay much attention to the teacher in class as they are still thinking about their bad morning. They take all of this out on their friends at school, which is just making matters much worse. Jane gets to work and is thirty-five minutes late, the doctor is livid and her co-workers angry as well for they had to do all the work in setting things up. The copy machine runs out of paper and Jane is almost in tears. She speaks unkindly to the clients and to her co-workers, which sets the day reeling into a living nightmare at the doctor's office. All of the inhabitants of this office become grouchy and unkind to one another. The childcare provider spends two hours trying to calm the three-year-old girl down and in the process pays less attention to the two-year-olds who are screaming for attention. The provider has a day filled with no grace whatsoever and takes it out on her husband upon his arrival home from work. She and her husband get into a huge fight, which sends her own children to their rooms for refuge from the storm.

Do you see how the lack of grace in one's life affects the lives of others as well? All because Jane forgot to set her alarm and got off on the wrong foot. We have all had days like this and we may not realize it, but it is affecting all of those around us and it trickles down. This is a lack of grace in one's life. It is important to pray for patience and grace in all our days so that our lives will run smoothly and positively. Here is an example of a day with grace.

Jane goes to bed a little early so she can get up early and sets her alarm for 5:30 a.m. The alarm goes off and rising slowly and stretching out her arms, she prays for a day filled with grace. Jane makes her way to the shower, gets a fresh bar of soap and enjoys a cleansing of the body for ten minutes. She then dresses in one of her beautiful sundresses and puts on her makeup. After the coffee is done brewing she spends another half hour reading the newspaper, drinking her coffee, and also eating a healthy breakfast. Jane makes her way down the hall to the bedrooms of her children and wakes them all up gently and lovingly. She proceeds to dress her three-year-old, all the while giving her tender kisses on the cheek. They all meet up in the kitchen, where breakfast is underway. The seven-year-old asks for lunch money and Jane explains to the boy that she is out of cash and he will have to make his own lunch but that she will help him. The fifteen-year-old eats his breakfast and then asks Jane if he may use the car tonight so that he and his friends can go to a football game. Jane tells him that she would not mind taking the group of boys to the game but that he cannot drive by himself until he gets his license, which, she reminds him, will be in one week. He smiles and says that is fine and helps clean up the mess from the milk that his little sister spilled all over the floor when dumping her sippy cup. Jane cannot find her keys and asks everyone to help her look for them, and the seven-year-old finds them in the basement. Jane praises him for finding them and they all get their jackets and head for the car. Jane realizes that she left the diaper bag on the kitchen table and walks back into the house to get it. Meanwhile, the seven-year-old is helping get his little sister strapped into her car seat. The fifteen-year-old thanks God that he remembered his homework and they all begin their journey down the road, telling jokes and laughing. The three-year-old giggles as her mom places her in the provider's arms and kisses her goodbye, thanking her childcare provider for all the hard work she does. The boys are dropped off at the school and Jane tells them that she left cookies by the refrigerator for them once they get their chores all done after school. She waves goodbye and the boys head into school with smiles on their faces, greeting their friends and their teachers. Jane stops by the donut shop and gets a dozen goodies for her co-workers and boss. She walks into the office and is there early so she proceeds to fill the copy machine with paper and makes coffee for all of them. When the rest of them arrive for work, she hands them the box of donuts and points to the coffee. Her boss thanks her for buying his favorite donuts, chocolate raised, and over donuts and coffee they begin to discuss their day and how they will work together. The clients are pleased at the service they get and all leave the office smiling. The doctor is happy, his employees are happy and everyone leaves the office at the end of the day feeling good about all that transpired. The childcare provider has a wonderful day and hugs her husband when he arrives home from work, then her entire family sits down in the living room in the evening to watch *The Wizard of Oz*. Jane picks up her three-year-old and is surprised to see that dinner has been made upon her arrival home. Okay, it is grilled cheese sandwiches, but how nice of her sons to help make dinner for all of them! THIS IS GRACE! MAN ALIVE! IS IT EVER! Do you see the difference? Jane prayed and asked God for grace and it was given to her on a silver platter! Not only did her day go smooth, it went smooth for everyone around her as well and everyone was happy. Does this sound like an unrealistic situation? Perhaps. Not all days go like this one, that is a given; however, when the day starts out, we are asked to open our hearts and take a moment for prayer. To ask God to turn the day into a graceful one and move smoothly through it.

When I was growing up, most of my days seemed like days without grace. My mother was a single mom, raising five children after my father passed away. I remember her being frantic a great deal of the time, stressing out over just about everything. I just wanted to hide downstairs in my bedroom and get away from it all, but I was called to come upstairs and help her in the kitchen. I dreaded that sometimes because I could feel her stress and it wasn't graceful in the least! I was like the seven-year-old peacemaker, trying to do everything I could to make sure things ran smoothly. A big responsibility for a little kid. How many of you can relate?

God doesn't want your life to be like this. He wants your life to run smoothly and free of the wrinkles that life oftentimes sends forth. Sure, there are lessons to learn in patience and in staying positive, but it is all done through God's grace. He doesn't have a problem with the way things run, for God knows that he planned everything out perfectly. He has the sun coming up at the time it should, the moon rising when it should, the oceans' tide ebbing as he wills it, and so on. God doesn't need an alarm clock, for he is there while we are sleeping and follows us around in our day, seeing how we ford along on our journey. He wants it to be done gracefully so that all we come in contact with along the way are greeted by us in a cheerful way. God is fluid, like a feather on the breeze, like a wistful cloud passing, it is all done with the most remarkable grace. Allow God's grace to wistfully carry you along on your path. Allow his grace to move so freely within you that all whom you touch along the way are graced as well. Rise above that rocky road and float freely as you were always meant to. Fill your life with God's grace and free yourself.

2 Corinthians 9:8—*And God is able to make all grace abound toward you, that you, always having all sufficiency in all things, may have an abundance for every good work.*

1 Peter 4:10—*Each one should use whatever gift he has received to serve others, faithfully administering God's grace in its various forms.*

Respect

Spirituality has everything to do with respect. Not only respecting God, but yourself and others as well. In this day and age, we have seen the breakdown of family values. We have seen the rising up of children against their parents and this is because we don't demand respect from them anymore. As a substitute teacher at a local elementary school, the junior and high school as well, I have seen the rising up of students against their teachers and have also seen this in the child/parent relationship. As a general manager of a restaurant, I saw this in the workplace with the teens I worked with. It is prevalent among adults as well as children. It is a breakdown and much attention needs to be focused on this if we are to turn this world around. In fact, it is out of hand.

So, what caused this breakdown? In my opinion, it started back in the seventies. This is about the time when so many parents decided to start working outside the home. Many mothers no longer wanted to just stay home and raise their children. They wanted a second income, equal pay and equal jobs. Didn't seem like such a bad idea at the time. Who wouldn't want a second income and a chance at getting out there into the real world, where one could be justifiably pleased with their accomplishments and career? Sounded great, and to this day, there are many women attorneys, doctors, teachers, you name it. Women are working and working well; however, with this comes a sacrifice. The sacrifice of the tightknit family unit. The mother role has landed in the lap of the childcare provider. How do I know? I worked as a childcare provider for ten years. I raised other people's children. I saw women and men coming to my house to pick their children up after a long hard day at work with the McDonald's bag in the car. Frequenting their homes on visits, I saw children eating in the living room, being thrown a burger and fries. Where the dining room used to be a time of gathering and socialization in the home, it had become an empty room with a table cluttered with bills. Parents from a double-income family have the money to purchase many nice things for themselves and for their children but the *things* have become the pacifier for the children. Less and less time is spent on teaching and nurturing the children and more time spent on making the big bucks. The sad thing now is, because the economy has turned up the juice due to the double-income family, there is no recourse but to work. Unless one parent makes enough money to support the children and the spouse, which is rare these days, then both parents need to work. There are exceptions to the rule. There are many women who work out of their homes and are able to be there for their children. More and more companies are providing childcare at the office. Also, there are many wonderful childcare providers who nurture and teach as a mother would and can love them nearly as much as the child's own parents. I ask that all parents seeking childcare do their homework and find such a provider. What has essentially happened is that both parents started working, less time was spent with the child, and the child lost out on the bonding and molding stages. It is vital to mold the child in his or her earliest years. It is a fact that more and more children are being given *things* to make up for the lack of attention they need. What happens then is that the child ends up spoiled rotten. How do I know? I LIVED IT! When I was in the childcare profession, I would greet the parents at my door, and the parent would hand the child over to me with a look on their face that expressed their longing to stay with their child. I heard the words the parent would say to the child, "It's all right, I will be back to pick you up soon, I promise," with all the love and kisses the child needed but the heart of the parent was breaking more than that of the child! Upon picking up their child, it would be a joyous reunion and come to find out, Mom or Dad had bought their child gifts while out for the day and Burger King as well. Yippee! I saw the child that I was caring for go from being a little angel respecting the rules of the house to running rampant all over the living room and the parent would do nothing about this. Discipline had fallen by the wayside. Why? Guilt! Mom and Dad feel a bit guilty about leaving their child at the daycare and the repercussions that followed were enormous! I saw little Johnny getting away with murder upon pickup time and I knew this was going on in their homes as well because I made visits to the parents' homes and saw it firsthand. Guilt!

I have never been so appalled at the lack of discipline children are receiving as when I worked as a para-educator with the local school district. I worked in the preschool and just when I thought I had seen enough in my childcare, the kids in the preschool amazed me even more! Man alive! I would continually ask myself, "What is this world coming to?!" There were a few children who were very well behaved, but the majority of them could have used a major dose of discipline. It was very difficult for me to work in this position at the school because there seemed nothing I could do about it all. It was extremely frustrating! Spare the rod, spoil the child. It was so apparent! I carried on in the school teaching the children and dealing with their behaviors as best as I could. I was not the parent, I was a teacher, and needed to follow the laws of the school, social services and what society expected of me as a teacher. Still, the pit in my stomach grew the more lack of discipline I saw. When I went to work at the high school as a substitute teacher, the pit in my stomach grew to the size of a cantaloupe. Man alive! I have never been treated with such a lack of respect in my life! These were the adults of the future. In the next couple of years, these children would be adults! Few of them displayed behavior even close to that of an adult. Scary! I would ask them to be quiet in class and they talked even louder. I would ask them to put away their Walkmans, and iPods and pay attention to what their work was to be in class that day and they would refuse. They talked back to me, they turned me away, they visited with their neighbor, they would walk in late to class, they would ask to use the restroom and never come back to the classroom. The list goes on. It is no wonder we are losing teachers! It starts at home, folks! It starts with good parenting!

In the case of the single mom or dad, my heart goes out to them. But my mother told me years ago that it only takes one good parent. My mother had to work after my father passed on and she was stuck raising the five of us. But she never stopped disciplining and she didn't buy us things to make up for the lack of her being there while at work. She spent time with us in the evening. Throughout our lives, she never stopped teaching us, nor did she stop disciplining. Many single parents are so tired at the end of the day that they fall into a chair and forego the responsibilities of parenting. The most important job a person will ever do on earth is parent. It is the most rewarding and most difficult job on earth, but it is the most important. If you cannot take on this type of responsibility, then do not have children!

There is a place in the Bible where Jesus speaks to his disciples about the signs that the coming times are near when Jesus will walk the earth again. He tells them that children will rise up against their parents. How true this is! They have become mouthy and terribly disrespectful! They do not know much about responsibility as they work a job and quit as though it is nothing to show up for work and they could actually care less. Why should they care? Their parents will give them what they want! That is their thinking. They do not fear their parents' reactions. Why should they? The children of today seem to be the ones in control, not the parents.

All right, are all children bad children? Not in the least, as a matter of fact, in each one of these children there is a calling out for some discipline and teaching in their lives. Children WANT this! Children need this. Are all parents bad parents? No! I know many good parents. Parents who put their children first and foremost above all things, with love, discipline and respect. There needs to be a respect for the child as well as a child's respect for their parents. It all works hand in hand.

God knew that children would turn against their parents, teachers and many other adults. This is why Jesus told the disciples what he did. Are we living in the days that he spoke of? Yes! Wake up, world! Take a good look around and notice what is going on! It is time to teach the children how to be good. It is time to teach the children how to behave and stop pussyfooting around with them. Do not fear your children, teach them! Do not expect your child to be your friend and do not try to be the child's friend. This comes after you have raised them! Be a parent! Do not end up being a product of the system, stand up to it and let your children know you are there for them, you believe in them and that you love them by disciplining them! If both parents must work to make a decent living, then do not compensate by buying your children so many things to make up for the lack of your not being there! This is such a terrible mistake! Spend quality time with them by reading to them at night, letting them help in the kitchen, watch a wholesome program with them and teach them about GOD. Teach them about Jesus. Teach and teach some more for as a parent your job is to teach your children! Hug them, love them, and respect them, for they will respect you and others in turn.

The respect you hold in your heart for God is likened to the respect your children will hold in their hearts for you. God should be respected as our Father in Heaven. He is our Father and he wants us to be good, just as parents, we want our children to be good. The way to glorify God and to respect him is to teach your children how to love themselves, love others and love him. In turn, they will grow to love you deeper than the deepest blue sea. It all starts with a spiritual and godly heart. How do you live a spiritual life in such a suffering world? By setting the example as a parent. The children of tomorrow are Heaven's Hope. Respect.

It is time for the elderly of the world to receive some respect as well. When I worked as a certified nurse's aide, I saw firsthand how many of the elderly are treated, not just by some of the nurses at the nursing home I worked at, but by my fellow nurse's aides and also by the residents' own family! I saw many of them being shuffled around as though they were cattle going to slaughter! These seniors are people! These seniors have lived full lives and have given of themselves in their day. They are filled with wisdom and we would do very well to listen to them and respect them for teaching us what they have learned. They are our grandparents, our uncles and aunts and many of them are our parents! These elderly people deserve more respect than what they are being given. Had it not been for them, we wouldn't be alive today! I do not see enough volunteers at senior centers, hospices or nursing homes. I do not see enough people holding doors open for them or allowing them to go before them in the line at the grocery store, or taking time to listen to what they have to say! Many of our seniors are failing in their health, and we should be there for them, not just because we care, but because this will be US in a few years and we would want the same treatment.

I remember when I was young, my mother was working for the Department of Social Services and was also a volunteer for the Area Agency on Aging in Pueblo, Colorado. I didn't know much about her job, but she was a social worker who did elderly placement. She would help the elderly find homes whether it be with a care giver or in a nursing home. I recall her coming home and speaking out loudly on the treatment of the seniors she came in contact with. She was appalled at what she had seen in the course of her days with Social Services. The elderly should be treated with respect. I have had some people tell me that not all elderly folks are nice and that not all of them should be treated nice, especially if they are not nice to others. Imagine yourself at the age of seventy and up! Imagine how you may start to feel as your health starts to decline. It is no day at the beach! Imagine being on multiple medications for all sorts of maladies and infirmities. Imagine being stuck in a wheelchair and pushed into a room and forgotten about. Imagine not having your mental senses as acute as they once were. If we put ourselves in the position of being elderly, I think there would be a double take. I understand how difficult it is for some family members to venture out to see their loved ones in nursing homes, it is not always a pretty picture. To see one's father, mother, grandmother failing in health and not up to par as they once were is very difficult. My own mother died of lung cancer and my siblings and I took care of her until the last couple of weeks of her life. It was not easy by any stretch of the imagination. If you think about your loved one and their feelings and their heart, then you will understand the need for your being there. The elderly should be respected, and even if they seem like they are going back to being like little children, well, so be it! Let them. Everyone ages in their own way, but that doesn't mean that they give up loving, or that they give up wanting to be loved. Even to sit with them for an hour is better than distancing yourself completely. The elderly deserve our respect. One day, you will also be elderly, wise and weary. You will also want respect. Teach this to your children as well, as children may not understand what it means to be elderly, but they do need to understand that it is important to treat these wonderful and wise folks with the utmost respect and dignity.

In closing this chapter, know that if growing spiritually means to love others, this means respecting others as well. Your boss, your parents, your teachers, all people in all walks of life and in all races and religions. If you are not respected as you feel you deserve to be, then set the example by treating those who may not respect you with the utmost respect. Be the example and treat people well, love them and understand they are human beings just as yourself. God will bless you so fully and you will gain the respect of the heavens. Respect God, respect all people.

Hebrews 12:9—*"Furthermore, we have had human fathers who corrected us, and we paid them respect. Shall we not much more readily be in subjection to the Father of spirits and live?"*

Leviticus 19:3—*"Each of you must respect his mother and father, and you must observe my Sabbaths. I am the LORD your God."*

Leviticus 19:32—*"Rise in the presence of the aged, show respect for the elderly and revere your God. I am the LORD."*

1 Peter 2:17—*"Show proper respect to everyone: Love the brotherhood of believers, fear God, honor the king."*

Suffering

Suffering comes in all shapes and sizes. One person's suffering cannot be measured by another's suffering. It is pain, whether it lies in the heart or the physical body. On your spiritual journey, you will be called upon to suffer, either in your own body or as a part of someone else's suffering.

Physical pain is something I know a great deal about as I suffer from asthma, allergies, migraines, arthritis, interstitial cystitis, type 1 diabetes, menopause, panic attacks, two heart conditions and a host of other ailments. The question is how to get through such suffering and do it gracefully, all the while keeping one's faith.

In this life, you will be made to suffer, in one form or another. There is an end to it, if you not only believe there can be, but you KNOW there can be. The extent of your suffering depends a great deal on how you face it. How you rise to meet the challenge and how you keep God as your focus. I have watched programs on television where an evangelist will lay his hands on someone suffering and immediately they are healed. Should we believe in this or is this some play on dramatics to get us to believe that this person can really, in fact, heal someone? Is this, in fact, real? Is this faith? I choose to believe. Now that doesn't mean I am sure; I just choose to believe. I don't actually KNOW that this person has been healed but by their expressions and by what I believe in, it is really quite miraculous! Suffering and healing go hand in hand and the reason one is there is for the other. Faith is the healer. How much faith you carry in your heart is vital for your healing. This is up to God, his timing and his will that you are. Some people have all the faith in the world and are never healed. Perhaps they lacked faith, perhaps God felt there was something they needed to learn, or others needed to learn in regard to their suffering. We may not understand why, but we must understand that God's plan is perfect and there may be reasons for that person's suffering to be prolonged. This could be to teach others compassion, to teach others about pain, about faith and about prayer.

For the longest time, I have been praying for God to heal me of my suffering. I have lost jobs because of neck injuries and because I am unable to do what I used to do in my employment due to these injuries. Also, due to the diseases and conditions that seem to be plaguing me. My own personal suffering is so great at times that there doesn't seem a way out, and it doesn't seem as though there is anyone out there who will understand the extent of my suffering. Everyone who suffers goes through this. It is a frustration which endures. But we need to believe and know that by enduring we will make it through. Why has God not healed me if I have so much faith in him and his healing miracles? Because it is not the right time. I believe that I am made to suffer because it is important for me to understand what others go through and how they are asked to endure as well. Had I not gotten the diabetes, I would never fully understand what a diabetic is made to endure. Had I not suffered in my neck injuries, I would never have learned as much about the nerves in the neck, the skeletal structure and how they are intertwined. I would never know what it is like to be on workmen's compensation or assistance. There is learning in suffering. The list goes on. It is important to learn the lessons in suffering, so that we may understand the pain others experience, and we also learn about the body, heart and mind. I have many friends who suffer from bipolar disorder. This is a life-altering illness! I have never experienced it myself, but do experience it through my friends and can see the extensive damage it can play in others' lives. Alcoholism is an illness. I have never been an alcoholic but I have seen in my own personal experiences with loved ones who were and are alcoholics the damage and suffering it can cause in relationships, in families, in the workplace. The list of suffering is endless in this world. From hunger to disease to inherited illnesses and so on. It is so important to remember that our suffering is just as great as another's. A hangnail to one person may be like leg cramps to another. We cannot expect others to take on our pain, but we can hope for friends and family members to be empathetic and understanding regarding our sufferings. It is also important to remember that people who suffer need people to talk to about their pain. An outlet, a release, and we should be understanding and listen to people. For when it comes down to our own suffering, we would also want that.

People have asked me why God would allow so much suffering in the world. People who have lost loved ones due to natural disasters or terrorism, or things which are so out of human control. I tell them that God takes people home to heaven instantly upon such a tragedy. God will at times sacrifice humans on earth to teach others about faith and compassion. People are called upon to learn about this through the loss of family members and friends. God is not mean, he just wants us to learn. People suffer pain so that they may learn faith in God. When a person suffers and is healed from their suffering, there is a dawning realization that there are two sides to every street. People suffer to see both sides of the street. There are bad things in life to teach us about the good. There is evil in this world so that we can learn about godliness. There is death in the world so that people will learn about life. There is an opposite to all things and in suffering, we are called upon to learn about physical and emotional healing.

Suffering does not only mean suffering physically, there is emotional suffering that people live with. Perhaps the worst suffering in the world is the suffering of the heart. When we lose loved ones we suffer grief. Grief can last a short time or it can last a lifetime. It depends on one's faith and how they view death. To those with a godly heart, death is just another doorway to life. In heaven, there is everlasting life and Jesus spoke about this quite a few times during his time on earth. We must remember that our suffering does not last. Even if you are not healed of your suffering in this lifetime, you will be healed of it in heaven. You have heard the expression that "This too shall pass," and it will! When I was in the hospital giving birth to my son Adam, this was a hard lesson to learn as I was in labor for almost thirty-six hours. It was the worst suffering I have ever experienced. I was a diabetic and the doctors didn't know this. I had never been tested for the diabetes while pregnant. After two days in the hospital with roller coaster contractions, I had to have an emergency C-section. Adam was fine and healthy weighing in at a hefty nine pounds, twelve ounces. By the thirtieth hour of labor, I had given up and was in so much pain that I asked God to take me home to heaven. I just couldn't take the pain anymore, I hadn't slept in two nights and hadn't eaten anything in about the same time. I was spent! I kept my faith though and just pleaded with God and prayed to him as every contraction came and went. I am very lucky to be alive now and the whole procedure was a miracle right down to Adam, whom I still consider a "miracle child." While suffering through childbirth, there is a light turned on in the mother's heart that says, "You will be fine, you will make it, and you will suffer only for a short time, all will be well." It is so hard to hang on to that thought when every contraction seems like a knife cutting into your gut. We make it through with our faith, our hope and our belief and knowledge that God knows exactly what he is doing and there is a reason for this suffering.

When someone is heartbroken and filled with grief at a given loss in their life, we can be a good friend by praying for them and standing by them throughout this grieving process. I have a friend who lost a granddaughter. This little girl was still a toddler and my friend was grief stricken when this precious gift of life was taken home to heaven. It seemed so unfair and so many of us, friends and family members, tried diligently to get our friend to heal from her grief. This does not always happen because people need their own time to grieve and one person cannot tell another how to get over the loss of a loved one and expect it to happen overnight. We can, however, be there for that person to comfort, love and support. It can take years to heal from grief and sometimes people never get over their grief. People who grieve must remember that heaven is a prayer away and there is no such thing as death for children and those with godly hearts, only life everlasting. It is important to also remember that we will all see our loved ones again.

In our spiritual growth, we are called upon to learn about suffering so that we can learn compassion. We are called upon to learn about faith. We are called upon to pray for those suffering, and also come to their aid with support and love. We will all suffer eventually, and we would want others to be there for us, so we need to empathize with others and try to feel their pain as much as possible. What you give to others will always come back to you.

This is a world of great suffering right now. We have suffering coming at us like gangbusters. In fact, the list is so long regarding the world's sufferings that it would take three more pages just to list them. Financial suffering is great. Our economy is suffering tremendously and people are being laid off from jobs where they toiled diligently, some for the majority of their adult lives. We have the threat of pandemics circling around us and terrorism has caused fear in our hearts, which also encompasses suffering. All of our fears cause suffering. In fact, believe it or not, it has become a topic of conversation in a great portion of our conversations throughout the day. We need to let much of this go, and take it straight to the heart of God through prayer. He is the one who will rid the world of suffering and also the suffering in people's personal lives.

Remember that suffering is God's way of teaching. Teaching lessons about compassion, faith and healing. Know that God is with you in your pain and suffering and that this too CAN pass. Pray for God to heal you from your suffering, never give up, cling to your hope and faith and you shall be healed! Pray for the sufferings of others so that they too, may experience the miraculous power of healing. Christ suffered for us, so that our sufferings would be healed through him.

2 Corinthians 1:3-4—*3 Blessed be the God and Father of our Lord Jesus Christ, the Father of mercies and God of all comfort, 4 who comforts us in all our tribulation, that we may be able to comfort those who are in any trouble, with the comfort with which we ourselves are comforted by God.*

Acts 3:16—*"By faith in the name of Jesus, this man whom you see and know was made strong. It is Jesus' name and the faith that comes through him that has given this complete healing to him, as you can all see."*

Good Deeds

Good deed doers of the world unite! Whoever said that good deeds will not get you into heaven? To this day, that continues to baffle me. Anyone who does good deeds and does them sincerely (sincerely being the operative word here), is also one who keeps Jesus in his or her heart. Doing good for others is something that only one with a godly heart can do. It is a blessed thing and you do not see evil people walking around doing good deeds, unless they are people trying to deceive by their good works. The people I know who do good deeds do them because they are filled with faith and compassion. They do these deeds out of the willingness of their heart and their love for their fellow man and their love for God. While walking on your spiritual journey, you must remember that it is your faith which is the basis for your salvation and the good deeds you do come from such a faith.

I have been the recipient of others' good deeds, I have also been the good deed doer as well, but I am reminded to not let my left hand know what my right hand is doing. This is spoken of in the Bible and it is an important thing to know. God loves his children on earth who give from their hearts, their time, their money, compassion and love. But to walk around boasting about your good deeds will completely dismiss what you have done altogether. It is better to not delve into doing good works than to do them and let everyone know about them. What is it to tell the world of your good deeds? Would it not be better to allow the recipient to tell the world? It is important to do nice things for people, but to remind yourself of your good works and to remind others takes your efforts and throws them into the wind, for God does not favor selfish pride in giving. You may as well not even do the deed at all.

The greatest givers on the earth are those who are more concerned with the person or persons being given to, rather than the focus on themselves for what they are doing. To be honest, when I receive an e-mail or phone call from someone in regards to their giving, I am put off. It all depends on their hearts and how and why they have chosen to give, but if someone tells me that they gave to so-and-so and pride themselves on the giving it turns my stomach upside down. The spiritual person does well by forgetting that which they have given and focuses on the next deed they can do to help another. To forget your own giving is godly! It doesn't become such a big thing when you do it all the time, it becomes part of who you are and people can see your giving without your advertising it.

When you listen to your godly heart, in your spiritual advancement, your heart will come up with all different ideas as to how to give. There are many ways in which to give your heart to others. A nice card to someone who is ill or feeling bad in some way is an easy way to give of yourself. To visit your neighbor with a plate of brownies in your hand for no reason at all is another way to give. There are so many ways to give of yourself that the list is just endless.

Offering money to friends in need is a wonderful thing; however, it may serve you sadly to loan your money. Many times the recipient of the money may not be able to pay you back and in the long run, this may cause a rift in your relationship. It is better to be a giver and not a lender. God sees your giving to others in a monetary sense and when you do this freely without asking for anything back, it is a blessed thing for the recipient, as well as for your own heart. To borrow money from others is never easy, as you want to pay them back quickly and sometimes this is not possible. Do not borrow money if you can help it. If a good friend or family members offers you the money freely, without condition, know that you have been truly blessed, as they will be. God will make sure that the giver is blessed, maybe not in a monetary sense, but God always sees to it that his deitous givers, those who give unconditionally without expecting anything in return, are blessed with many wonderful things.

It is so good to get out into the community and volunteer. There are lists through the local chamber of commerce offering volunteer opportunities. Most hospices are always in need of volunteers, as are hospitals, nursing homes, developmental disability organizations, libraries, and almost all schools welcome volunteers. Those who have the time to give of themselves, those who are capable, are in great need. Animal shelters would welcome volunteers as well. I speak of helping others in this book, but animals need our help as well and anyone who can get out there and help out their local animal shelter would be appreciated greatly!

My mother, who was given the Sunshine Award in Pueblo, Colorado, as volunteer of the year, made me proud! She would tell me while growing up that the most important thing you can do on this earth is give of yourself to your community. She would say that we are here on this earth to give to others and to give back, before we go home to heaven. In her life, she gave more back to the world than anyone I have ever met. John

Denver is another whom I admire for his giving. He did this unselfishly and with his entire heart, in many ways. He set an example for so many of us. It amazes me to hear others speak of the great givers of this world in hateful ways as "goody-goody's" and "do-gooders" and there is such a negative connotation with all of that. I believe a lot of this is due to jealousy and insecurity on the part of the "slammer." There is nothing wrong with being a goody-goody. In fact, it is he who shall reap the rewards of heaven. God recognizes what people do unselfishly and it is to be commended! There are so many ways to give! I had a friend who had breast cancer and beat it. While she was going through chemotherapy treatments her friends rallied together and shaved their heads in thoughtfulness to her losing her hair. They all stuck together and this meant more to her than anything else! Spending time with people does not take money and this is another thing that people can do to make others feel good. Showing your love for someone does not mean buying them gifts constantly. It means being there for them in heart, in spirit, in love. I have seen certain celebrities give of themselves in huge ways by buying cars and expensive material things for people. They can do this because they have the income by which to do it, to advertise this is something that tugs at my heart, however. It makes those who cannot give like this feel awful and boasts on the celebrity. I don't necessarily blame the celebrity but I do blame the media for its constant praise and promoting of this. Do not feel bad if you cannot give to others in such a way, just do your best by loving those around you. The best gift you can give to another is your love and your compassion. Your smile, which comes from your sincere heart, is the greatest gift on earth. Walk your journey knowing that you are a giver and give to all in your path, whether it be your smile, your laughter, your strength or your deitous and kind words. Blessings come to the giver who gives unselfishly and without boasting.

Matthew 6:1-4—*1 "Take heed that ye do not your alms before men, to be seen of them: otherwise ye have no reward of your Father which is in heaven. 2 Therefore when thou doest thine alms, do not sound a trumpet before thee, as the hypocrites do in the synagogues and in the streets, that they may have glory of men. Verily I say unto you, They have their reward. 3 But when thou doest alms, let not thy left hand know what thy right hand doeth: 4 That thine alms may be in secret: and thy Father which seeth in secret himself shall reward thee openly."*

Heaven's Heart

Much recognition is owed to heaven. Without heaven, we would have nothing to go home to, we would not see our loved ones after this life, and we would not gain the assistance we need here on earth as we walk our journey. Are there really angels that watch over and protect us? We would all like to think so. In my heart, I know it is true.

What is meant by the term "Heaven's Heart?" It is the empathy, the love, the guidance, the inspiration and the protection we receive from what we cannot see which is good and godly. It is the light that shines within all of us who are spiritual and good. The belief and the knowledge that there is a place where only goodness dwells, where colors are brilliant, where nature is all encompassing. If you are filled with faith, then there is a vision of this place, this peace, living within you. Many people do not understand what heaven is all about.

I remember watching a television special the other night where a certain well-known celebrity/reporter was interviewing certain religious individuals from all faiths about their beliefs regarding heaven. Shocking to say the least! MAN ALIVE! I sat in my chair, cozy and relaxed and listened to the differences of beliefs in all these people, in all these faiths, with my mouth agape. There was an evangelistic leader in our community, who runs one of the largest chains of churches in the United States, who pointed up towards the sky when asked where he thought heaven was. Not that there was anything wrong with this. Let's see, if we are on the earth, and we point upwards towards the sky, then we are pointing toward the vast space above us. Since there are people all over the world who believe the same thing, then if you think about it, heaven would be all over space, out there in the vast, empty cauldron of space where universes reach beyond universes. So then, which direction is it? Towards Mars? Toward the moon and north? The physics pertaining to the location of heaven are beyond our comprehension. It is much simpler than that and yet, not really. Because we live in a three-dimensional world, it is difficult for our monkey brains to grasp the next dimension, but I can tell you this, heaven is not out there in space and you cannot use a roadmap to find it. In the Bible, in most scriptures relating to heaven, you will read the words "up" or "above" and that we are "under," and so on. Spiritual heaven, in fact, lives within each and every one of us. Getting in touch with heaven is not difficult in the least. It all depends on how deeply your desire is to find it. When you leave this earth, you will go within. To the farthest reaches of your wonderful and dear imagination, to the place where your dreams live, to the place where your greatest and most wonderful visions of things exist. To find heaven, look within your heart, for your spiritual heaven is inside, not outside. There is a quote from one of my favorite author/poets, Ralph Waldo Emerson, that says, "Though we travel the world over to find the beautiful, we must carry it with us or we will find it not." When I first read this, it touched me deeply for he, in his glorious words, described heaven. You cannot find heaven outwardly if you do not carry it inwardly. When a person on earth dies, how in the world do they travel within themselves? It is something that only God knows. But upon the last beat of one's heart begins the journey into the beautiful, glorious light of one's own heart. Those who have had near-death experiences will oftentimes speak of the tunnel they travel through in such a peaceful state. Of course, there is no way I can tell you for sure, but it strikes me as being the center of oneself in which they are traveling. Going within, for isn't that where all good things live? Within your heart? God lives there. I believe the heart is more than just an organ that keeps us alive on earth, it is what you feel when you fall in love, when you receive a blessing that brings tears to your eyes, even when you are sad, for it is the center of all feeling. Living one's life on earth is all about feeling, as is living one's life in heaven. You travel straight back to your center, your heart. Heaven's Heart is also where the imagination thrives. Your imagination is where God lives as well, and so many scoff at this! People have their own ideas about the imagination, but without it, we wouldn't have the dreamers of the world. God bless the dreamers! IMAGINATION! It is one of the greatest gifts on earth! Imagination is the basis for all true vision. One can imagine what heaven is all about, bingo! If you can imagine it, then you can experience it. One day, when we go home to heaven, we will see all that existed and thrived in the most beautiful realms of our imagination. This is why I do not believe that everyone's heaven looks or is exactly like another's. How could it be? That would be like telling people that heaven is concrete and everyone goes to a place which resembles Colorado. Sure, Colorado is a heavenly place on earth, but many people do not desire living in the mountains, some people want to live near the ocean and to them, California might be their vision of heaven. God is a people pleaser, and you will receive your blessings after this life on earth in a place where your heart finds the most peace.

I have studied near-death experiences and believe in them fully, as I too had such an experience. Mine was more like an out-of-body experience as I did not die on earth, but I did travel to this place called heaven and it was all about feeling. I didn't receive the visuals in a geographical sense, but the feeling was extremely intense and filled with a love that is indescribable. This is why so many who have had a near-death experience have difficulty explaining the feelings upon arrival in heaven after they are brought back to earth. It is profound! How can one come back to earth after having experienced such a gift and describe a feeling and a sense of peace that doesn't exist here on earth? I do believe that we all want to find such a heaven on earth, but heaven itself is the blessing you receive for your searching of it while on earth.

Heaven's Heart is the heart of all beings who dwell there. The spirits in heaven are always with us. They love us, they guide us, they protect us and they are constantly praying for us. Just because you may not see these spirits doesn't mean they do not exist. Our lives do not end with earth, they continue on, and we don't stop working upon leaving the earth; however, the work we do in heaven is without stress, without suffering, without those long hours that make one weary. It is joyous. If you enjoy doing for others on earth, you will without a doubt be called upon to do unto others in heaven. Imagine, if you will, living a life without pain, stress, suffering, and being able to do things that make other people happy all the time!! Man alive! Heaven is here for us, to use to our blessed advantage. Make use of Heaven's Heart, for it is yours for the taking! Talk to the angels for they are with you! Pray for the angels who watch over you. Love them dearly for they are here for your own well being and peace within. They not only live within your heart, they live all around us! It is just too bad that more people do not have faith in all of this, for surely, they are at a disadvantage on earth.

Heaven's Heart beats for us all, if only we would wake up and pay attention to what the spirits are saying to us. To do this, all one needs to do is to ask God to bless them with angels to watch over them and be their companions. You have the power to unleash the most beautiful spirits that live within you so that they can do for you. They are there for YOU! Just as God is. They live to serve because they love to serve. On your spiritual journey, take many fine moments to pray for Heaven's Heart. Watch your life take a turn, as signs are revealed to you from heaven. You are the one who can do this; all it takes is a prayer, and much faith. God wants you to become a very spiritual being on earth, and he will not give up on you. Find Heaven's Heart within and all around, and you will start noticing beauty and goodness in the things which you never realized before. You will become a part of Heaven's Heart as you are pulled into its light, its goodness and the power of freedom forever. No, heaven does not exist in space 100 million light years away…heaven lives inside YOU! If Jesus lives in your heart, then that is where heaven lives.

I was going to give a scripture in affirmation for this chapter but decided that I would have to write out or copy and paste the entire Bible.

All Things Spiritual

As you move along in your spiritual journey, you will start to recognize that your awareness has been heightened. You will see that you are living more and more in a spiritual way. Everything you do will be done with spiritual thought and recognition. I am not saying that you become this perfect human being, but you will be more aware of things that you say or do that are not along spiritual lines. When you lose your temper, you will recognize it and stop and think about how you should react, instead of slamming yourself for how you just reacted. This is all part of the learning. You also become more aware of others around you and their spiritual levels as well. Be careful, as you should never judge another, but you will be able to recognize on which part of the spiritual ladder they stand and have climbed. Do not be too hard on anyone who hasn't climbed the way you have. In fact, one of the most spiritual things you can do on earth is to bring along others as you climb. Not an easy thing to do, for those who have not placed a foot on the spiritual ladder may not listen to you. You run the risk of losing family members and friends as you grow spiritually. You transform and not all will love your transformation. Be cautious as to how you speak to others about your transformation and be gentle with hearts which are ignorant of spirituality. There is a way to share God with others, but it doesn't mean to rush madly into the world and choke people with your words of wisdom. Setting an example in all you say and do, making careful choices as to what you want to get involved in, is important. The best way to witness to people isn't by shoving a Bible in their faces. The best way is to be godly in all your ways. Believe me, they will all notice and those who don't like what they see are jealous, insecure about their own lack of spiritual growth, or do not quite understand it all. Have patience with them and teach them through kindness, patience and love. Bring up to them only things which their own hearts can understand and accept. Do not gag people on God!

A friend of mine was working as a teacher in a school. She sat down in the teachers' lounge to eat her lunch one day and sat at a table with co-workers when the subject of another teacher came up. The rest of the teachers started to gossip maliciously about this teacher and his antics. My friend sat there with her mouth gaped open while listening to all of this trash. She wanted to leave but then again, she ran the risk of being ostracized for being the only one not supporting this chat. So she sat there and decided to mention to the others that it was unfair for them to be speaking in front of each other about a person who could not defend himself. To her amazement, one of the teachers told her that she was right. Instead of being put down for her lack of support regarding their negative words, she was praised by all of them and they embraced her with positive feelings and words. They all agreed that she was right and decided not to speak about this fellow teacher anymore. My friend set a positive example and taught them all something about discretion and confidentiality; also that gossip hurts everyone, not just the person being spoken of.

Setting an example means to speak out about your own feelings but it doesn't mean to step all over the feelings of someone else. For example, while watching a football game, I noticed that there were many beer commercials which were enticing the viewer to buy such a brand of beer. I find this offensive. I told my friend, who is a beer drinker. He didn't understand why I would find this so offensive. In my spiritual heart, God tells me that alcohol is very bad. In my own personal life, I have experienced unpleasant happenings related to alcohol. It destroys families, ruins relationships and it kills. Why should I enjoy commercials that entice people into buying such a horrendous thing! Well, I made my feelings known, but it hasn't stopped my friend from drinking beer. So be it. However, my voice has spoken and I made a point. He knows where I stand with it all, but I will not control his actions. He must make it a point to stop drinking as I cannot do this for him. A spiritual person can voice their opinions, there is nothing wrong with this, but do not always expect a sympathetic ear. Not everyone is on the same spiritual level regarding the ways of the world. Controlling others is not godly. Offering advice gently is, and so is expressing your spiritual viewpoint. Arguing about God is not healthy, but sharing about God is. Keep an open mind and an open heart. Like I said in a previous chapter, religion is different from spirituality. Arguing will never prove your point to another, it will only cause and create dissension. If you are a Christian and you are having a conversation with a friend who is a Buddhist regarding your religious views, do you really think you are going to change the mind of the Buddhist when his culture is all about Buddhism? No way! However, there is nothing wrong with sharing with him how you feel about your own beliefs. There is nothing wrong with mentioning that you are a Christian and believe that

Jesus Christ is the Son of God. There is nothing wrong with sharing how you worship, where you attend church or anything regarding your own personal beliefs, but to argue your point regarding salvation with this person is going to be futile, I can tell you that right now. Be a friend to this person, love him and respect him and he will see right away that you are a spiritual being with great love in your heart for others. This is the way to show someone your spiritual heart. Share what you feel comfortable in sharing and know that God watches and hears everything you say and do. Will you ever turn this person around to your way of believing? Maybe, maybe not. But you will most assuredly be rewarded for your good and godly heart. Spirituality isn't about arguing or fighting, it is about sharing.

Every single thing you say, do, think and feel should have a godly focus. When you find that your life is not going the way you think it should, pray about it. When you lose your patience, pray about it. When you say something which hurts another's heart, pray about it. Remember that you are meant to learn lessons and the path of spirituality is filled with lessons. No matter how many times you wander off the path, if you keep God in your heart, a light will shine which will lead you back onto the correct path again.

Let your ways be good, and forever kind. Pray for forgiveness and know that God loves you so much that no matter how you stray at times, you are loved and will always be made whole again.

Colossians 1:9-10—9 *"For this reason we also, since the day we heard it, do not cease to pray for you, and to ask that you may be filled with the knowledge of His will in all wisdom and spiritual understanding; 10 that you may walk worthy of the Lord, fully pleasing Him, being fruitful in every good work and increasing in the knowledge of God."*

Thinking Like Jesus

Jesus. The perfect being. God in human form. Brought into the world immaculately, taken from the world suffering, resurrected in God's glory. There has never been another being created in comparison. This was God's only begotten Son, sent to the world to heal, to teach, to love and to die for us all so that we may live. His thought was perfect, his ways were perfect, and to this day, he lives. He lives in heaven and he lives in all of those who keep his heart in theirs.

In your spiritual ways, you are asked by God to think like Jesus. You are asked to live as much like Jesus as you can, through faith and prayer. In all your ways, you should remember Jesus and what he would do in a given situation. In all situations. Your actions are important just as his were. Your mind and your heart are important as his were. Your life is important as his was. Yes, he was the most important spirit ever sent to earth, for without Jesus and the life he lived, we would not have a redeemer. We would not be forgiven for our sins had he not lived and suffered in death.

How can one go about their lives thinking as Jesus did? By remembering Jesus in all ways. A godly mouth is a must, a godly heart is the key. What we say to others leaves a lasting mark on the world. What you speak, speak in godly terms. What you think, think in the godliest of ways. Put Jesus in the forefront of your heart and mind when you go about your daily life. When you are confronted by those who do not put Jesus first, you do not need to partake of their conversations, you do not need to give in to their way of being. Pray continually, love continually, forgive continually.

In my own life, there has been more than one occasion which would cause anyone to lash out. I have not always been treated kindly by others. None of us have. When these types of situations come about, instead of lashing out at those who you feel do you wrong, pray for them. Turn away from them, instead of being pulled into their darkness. Recently, I had a friend call me on the phone. She began to tell me about how unfairly she had been treated by the couple who sold her the car she recently purchased. She was livid! She may have had every right to feel angry but my advice to her was to remember Jesus. She stayed on the other end of the phone line, pausing a bit, but I continued on to tell her that the couple that sold her the car she was driving may not be where she is spiritually and she needed to remember that praying for others is key. She was treated rudely, yes. She had been treated unfairly, yes. But to set an example in the world means to turn away from the ugly side of things and embrace all that is forgiving and beautiful. What she really must learn is that by harboring all of this hatred for this couple, she is only doing herself and them a disservice. The anger and contempt felt in this situation breeds more anger and contempt on the part of all. It becomes a no-win situation. As she listened she agreed that what I was saying made sense and said she would try to deal with all of this in a kinder way.

Here is another story of true forgiveness. I had a friend who worked in a preschool. Her boss lacked quite a bit in people management skills. She would treat her subordinates in ways that were very unprofessional. There was a day when this friend went into work and this boss was in a foul mood. As the day progressed, the boss would go around the room picking on the teacher's aides and she just didn't let up. This not only made the aides a nervous wreck, it kept them from focusing on the children and their attention was being paid to the boss as they all walked along on pins and needles. After a couple of hours of this, my friend had had quite enough of the badgering and lost her patience with her boss. What ensued were righteous words to the boss about her lack of discretion in front of the children and how my friend and her fellow aides could not focus on the work while the badgering in front of all was taking place. My friend rose up and spoke loudly regarding the boss's actions. In defense, the boss pointed her finger toward the door and told my friend that this was *her* preschool and that there was the door if my friend chose to leave if she couldn't handle the stress. My friend sat there for a moment and contemplated walking out. She really had every right to at that point. But she needed the job and had rent to pay so she stayed. After the class time was over, my friend walked over to the office and tapped on her boss's door. The boss let her in and there they quietly discussed the situation that had just passed. Both listened to the other as they professionally hashed over the situation. In fact, the boss praised my friend for coming in and discussing all of this with her professionally. Apologies were made and from then on, there was a great deal of respect between both parties for the rest of the school year. Forgiveness and patience for others is key in work situations. Harmony will not be present unless all parties are willing to let go of their pride and their anger and discuss things calmly, forgiving as they move along. Forgiveness heals hearts and it builds respect. Forgiveness is righteous! If one thinks like Jesus, then forgiveness is put into place.

FORGIVENESS is the path to peace. Never ever forget that as long as you walk your spiritual path. Patience is another very important thing. When you are in a situation that is tumultuous, and you feel yourself beginning to boil on the inside, take a deep breath and pause. Face the situation calmly, and remember who you are! You are a spiritual being who has learned to forgive others and yourself. Anger begets hate. Hate is not the tool of Jesus and it is not the tool of GOD!

Jesus was a fighter, for righteousness' sake. Yes, he told people off. But not in a way that was hateful, but in a way that was righteous. What does it mean to be righteous? There is a difference between self-righteous and righteous. Self-righteous means to go about your life believing that your way is the only way. Man alive! Does this cause problems all over the place! Everyone on earth experiences this, either in themselves or others. How many times has someone approached you with a self-righteous attitude? It doesn't seem like there is any room for budging where self-righteousness is concerned. It is more than likely the number one cause for dispute—more than any other. It involves pride and stubbornness. One of the things you will notice in your heart as you climb this ladder of spirituality is the falling away of self-righteousness. People can be down right hateful when their opinions and pride are attacked. This is because they cannot let go of it. Righteousness, on the other hand, is the defending of godly things. It also means to listen to what others have to say and to keep an open heart regarding another's viewpoint. Let me give you an example of righteousness.

A man is married to a woman who is very godly. But the husband is not godly in the least. They are having troubles in their marriage. The husband has cheated on his wife and has been lying to her and also drinking heavily behind her back. When the woman confronts him about this, she mentions prayer and going to Christian counseling. The husband blurts out to her that he no longer wants to hear about prayer and anything pertaining to God. The woman, in defense of her righteous beliefs, towers above him as he is sitting on the couch and lays into him. She defends God and tells this husband of hers that if he does not change his ways, he is heading in a downward spiral. She speaks up for God and for the marriage, stating that the only way to regain anything loving in this marriage is to turn to God. She is angry, but her anger comes from God himself and she can feel this in her heart. She knows that this is her righteous side coming through and thus continues to lay into him about the right way to heal this marriage. This is not self-righteous, for she is not giving her own opinions but rather God's firm stance on goodness and light. In her anger she has become righteous. When Jesus went to the temple in Jerusalem and saw the merchants selling their wares in the holy place of worship, he lost his temper, but it was in a righteous way. He upturned tables and shouted out to the merchants how they should not destroy God's holy temple by selling their wares within its confines. This was righteous. It is the same thing when you are speaking out in a godly way about what is right in the eyes of the Lord.

Think like Jesus. Forgive when forgiving is needed but speak out righteously when necessary as well.

When stuck in traffic, think before you speak, especially when others are in the car with you! Do not cuss out the driver in front, beside or behind you, this does not set an example of godliness. In fact, this teaches those in the car with you to do the same. The poor little children who end up hearing what their parents are saying! Set an example! Pray for those on the road who leave you seething, pray for the ones who do not drive as you would like them to, pray for everyone! Pray for the people you do not know for you may not know their circumstances and what causes them to drive as they do. If you end up doing or saying something which is hateful or hurtful, and you recognize it right away, speak out loud about this. Say, "Ooops, I should not have said that and I am sorry." Apologize to those around you and to God. It is far greater in the heart of heaven to receive an apology from a sinner, than for heaven to have an entire army of those who never sin. If you think about it, everyone sins, right? A time or two or three in their life. Multiple times actually. There is no perfect person. You are perfect in your imperfection, as long as you recognize your own sin and ask God to forgive.

Think like Jesus. In all ways, in all your actions as well. Be cautious about what you watch on the television and what music you listen to. Be cautious about how you live your life, and ready yourself for change. Be careful about the friends you choose. Stand up for God and turn away from those who do ungodly things, no matter the peer pressure, no matter the circumstance. Be careful about living self-righteously, and forcing your own opinions on others. Be patient with those around you and remember that they have a path to follow as well. Help them move up and onto the ladder of spirituality. Never forget that you are being watched over and listened to. You are also being guided and loved by the heavenly hosts. Be honest in what you do, in all your ways. Think about giving unconditionally and not for a price. Do not loan, be a giver. Volunteer your time to others. Love children as you love the elderly. Discipline your children, be a friend at all times to strangers. Smile at those who frown, teach by loving all. Remember the child in your heart, and think like Jesus, for he is your savior, your light, he is God. Bless you on your spiritual journey.

John 3:16—*"For God so loved the world that he gave his one and only Son, that whoever believes in him shall not perish but have eternal life."*

Man Alive!

Look at all the needy, the selfish and the greedy,
Oh Lord, I just can't take it, MAN ALIVE!
This world could use great healing, not murder, rape and stealing,
The lands are in an uproar, MAN ALIVE!
I wake with broken heart, for a world that just can't start,
To see the end of killing, MAN ALIVE!
It's so hard to live, in a world that can't forgive,
We need to find the truth here, MAN ALIVE!
When will fighting cease, when will man know peace,
It seems that it's all endless, MAN ALIVE!
Self-righteous cold debaters, so many ruthless haters,
So very disappointing, MAN ALIVE!
Some children's hearts are lacking, they're in the schools attacking,
Oh Lord, we need your glory, MAN ALIVE!
Families needing mending, hypocrites pretending,
Faith is fading swiftly, MAN ALIVE!
When will all embrace, the love of godly grace,
Why do they turn away, Lord, MAN ALIVE!

"They turn away, my child, for such ignorance runs wild,
And the coming times are here now, man's alive!
For more and more are turning, to a faith so filled with burning
Of a passion which is fruitful, man's alive!
Don't be disappointed, for the Holy One's anointed,
Will be seen among the many, man's alive!
Though the world looks grim, there is always faith in HIM,
For the Son of God is coming, man's alive!
If the world seems dreary, there is hope there for the weary,
For I have not forsaken, man's alive!
Look now toward the day, when all hate shall pass away,
It is not long in coming, man's alive!
Pray now for the yearning, of the faithful's sweet returning,
It is soon to be forever, man's alive!
For all who turn to me, with glory's light upon them see,
Heaven's Heart is waiting, man's alive!"
God's blessings shine upon the man who loves the dawn,
And this, my dear, for all who are alive!"